ALEXANDRIA
THE SUNKEN CITY

ALEXANDRIA
THE SUNKEN CITY

WILLIAM LA RICHE

PHOTOGRAPHY BY
STEPHANE COMPOINT / SYGMA

WEIDENFELD & NICOLSON
LONDON

THE GOD ABANDONS ANTONY

…At midnight, when suddenly you hear
an invisible procession going by
with exquisite music, voices,
don't mourn your luck that's failing now,
work gone wrong, your plans
all proving deceptive – don't mourn them uselessly:
as one long prepared, and full or courage,
say goodbye to her, to Alexandria who is leaving.
Above all, don't fool yourself, don't say
it was a dream, your ears deceived you:
don't degrade yourself with empty hopes like these.
As one long prepared, and full of courage,
go firmly to the window
and listen with deep emotion,
but not with the whining, the pleas of a coward;
listen – your final pleasure – to the voices,
to the exquisite music of that strange procession,
and say goodbye to her, to the Alexandria you are losing.

–C.P. CAVAFY
(translated by Edmund Keeley and Philip Sherrard)

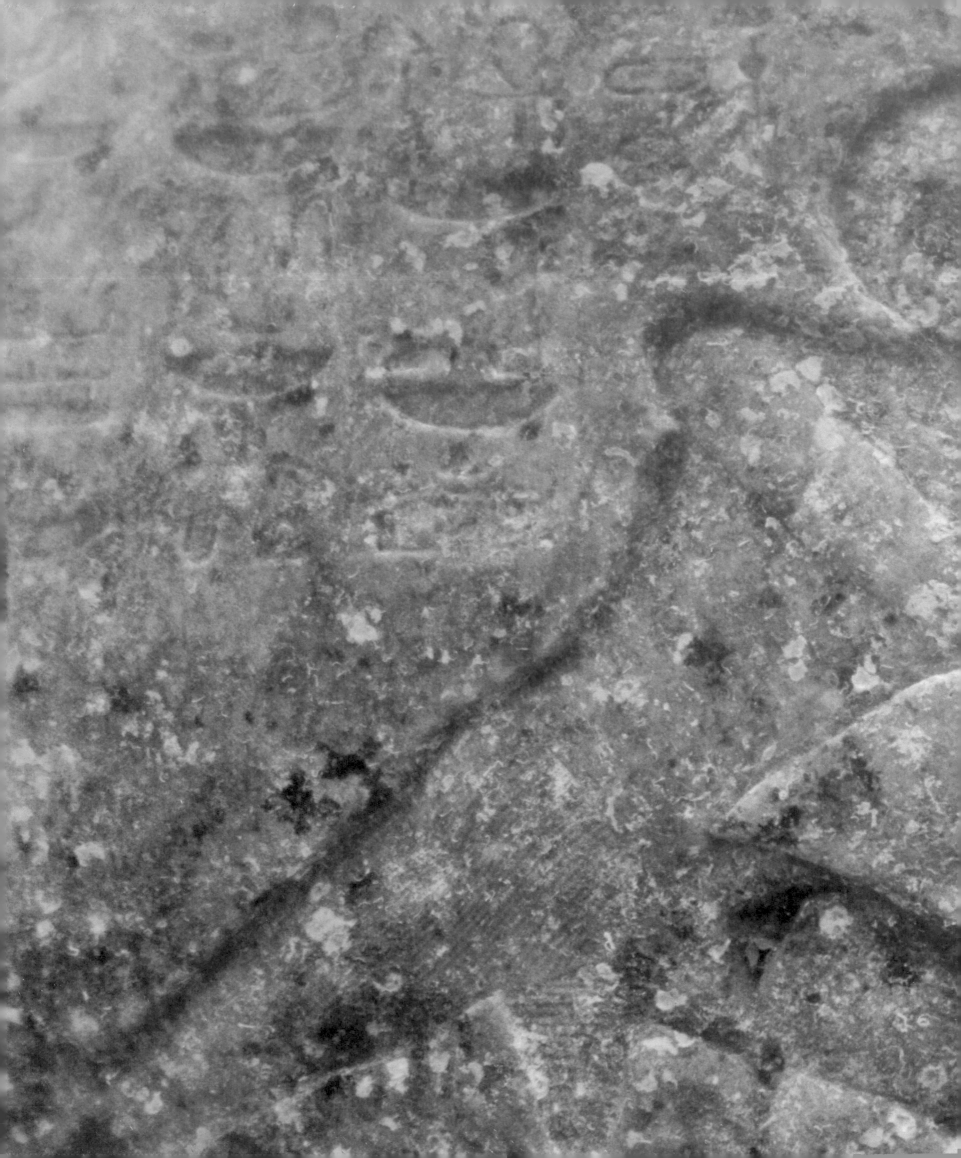

THE DRAMA OF
OCTOBER FOURTH

The sea, at Alexandria, rises up in the clear light of October fourth, 1995. It shatters, wave after wave, against the sea wall of the great, crescent-shaped Corniche. Passengers in several of the cars moving west along this northern edge of Egypt are wondering, this morning, if he can succeed – if Dr. Jean-Yves Empereur and his French-Egyptian team of archaeologists and divers actually can remove a massive, two-thousand year-old sculpture from so turbulent a sea. Among the more confident of these passengers is Empereur's fellow scientific coordinator of the project, Dr. Nicolas Grimal, head of the French Institute of Oriental Archaeology in Cairo. Others, less familiar with Empereur's abilities and therefore possibly more apprehensive, are the Head of Alexandria's Greco-Roman Museum, the Chairman of Egypt's Supreme Council of Antiquities, and the nation's Minister of Culture. Their destination is Fort Quayt Bey, a fifteenth-century stone structure built on the site of the ancient lighthouse which had been one of the Seven Wonders of the Ancient World. The lighthouse had occupied the very tip of the peninsula which once had been an island, and the name of which has been, since Homer's time, 'Pharos'. The huge tower which had stood there for so long, and which had shared with the island the name of 'Pharos', had risen to a height of perhaps four hundred feet. From its summit, forty storeys above earth and sea, a perpetual fire could be seen by ships seventy miles away. From the Fourth Century of the Common Era (A.D.), when it was already seven centuries old, the Pharos began to succumb to a series of earthquakes and, bit by bit, through the next millennium, tumbled, with its attendant sculptures, into the Mediterranean.

Now Empereur and his team – in what is the largest underwater archaeological excavation the world has ever seen – have begun a campaign that, in its first months, will rescue from the sea floor and several feet below it, the first three dozen sculptures and architectural pieces – among more than two thousand he has identified – blocks which date back to one of the

Pages 10-11: Block of calcite showing the pharoah Sethi I making offerings to the Gods.

Following page: View of the Eastern part of the Alexandria port, showing the mosque of Abou Abbas Al-Moursi, constructed between 1928 and 1945 and situated between Fort Quayt Bay and the city centre.

greatest civilizations of Antiquity, to the Hellenistic dynasty of the Ptolemies, and beyond. Founded by Alexander himself in the year 332 Before the Common Era – near the mid-point in time between the first unification of Upper and Lower Egypt and the present day – Alexandria was the Manhattan of the Ancient World. Like Manhattan, it was built near the mouth of a great river – the Canopic Mouth of the Nile. Like Manhattan, it became a major harbour on a great sea. Like Manhattan, it received huge and varied populations: Egyptians, Greeks, Jews, Italians, Sub-Saharan Africans, immigrants from the Levant, even Buddhists from India were among its million souls. Like Manhattan, Alexandria was laid out on a rectangular grid plan, for Alexander had charged his architect, Dinocrates of Rhodes, to create an urban matrix of encompassing order, to accommodate a vast variety of inhabitants with no hierarchical distinction. There were palaces to be sure – at one point one quarter of the city was incorporated into a royal enclave – and there were the seats of great institutions, but the whole city was not organised around a single centre. Like Manhattan, Alexandria possessed in its plan the potential for creating – and for endlessly recreating – a multitude of centres, as the make-up and values of the populace evolved.

The idea of Hellenism was that of including the universe within the Greek possibility.

The Hellenistic World included those lands – from the Western Mediterranean to parts of Afghanistan and India – where, in spite of Alexander's death, the Greek language and Greek culture continued to be practised and revered, even though the great majority of the inhabitants of those lands were not Greek by birth.

'I specialised in the Hellenistic World,' Empereur has said, 'because to my eyes it represents the

18th century carving of the small lighthouse, or lantern, of Alexandria's old port. A : small lighthouse. B: ruins of Ptolemy III's famous library. C: from the Bokkir castle. (Jean-Yves Empereur's private collection.)

explosion into realised achievement of the Greek World, and a moment of History when the citizen, while remaining citizen of a city, becomes a true citizen of the world, of the Greek World, which is to say, the entire known world of that epoch.'

Little of Hellenistic Alexandria is left on the surface of the land. Unlike Rome, the skin of the earth has not been peeled back to reveal the lost grandeur. The burgeoning nineteenth and twentieth centuries predominate in the architecture which occupies the city's surface.

On the platform lies the crane used to lift the massive blocks out of the water.

Earthquakes and the subsidence of the earth have consigned more than the Pharos to the sea: The palaces of the last of the rulers of the Ptolemaic Dynasty, Cleopatra VII, and that of her Roman consort, Mark Antony, now lie on and beneath the harbour floor with so much else of moment: the remnants of temples, government buildings, the principal market, the royal marina lie there also – and shards of the sculptures, architectural carvings and mosaics that had adorned them. Coupled with what lies beneath the buildings on dry land, and what is buried beneath the sands

along the coast from Aboukir to Alamein, the region of Alexandria is perhaps the greatest under-explored archaeological opportunity in the Mediterranean Basin. Jean-Yves Empereur is more aware of this than anyone else, and the challenge of October fourth is to create, in the teeth of the rising wind and the roiling sea, beneath the gaze of the czars of culture and the world's assembled press, a master demonstration of the rescue of a god.

The Emergence Of The Torso

The wind continues to rise, and, in the sea near Fort Quayt Bey, the divers in black wet suits circle a submerged prey like sharks. A huge barge waits near them, its deck pitching like that of a carrier on a day when no landings will take place. Still, Empereur is determined that the large carved stone his team has descended to secure will end this day in the dry October air. A chain from the barge's winch is suspended over the water. Two divers attempt to attach cables from the chain to the submerged object. They fail. The barge continues to pitch, and the winch's great chain swings menacingly near the divers, and near the cameramen, bobbing precariously in a rubber boat only several feet away.

The Minister of Culture is received, with his entourage, by the French Ambassador on the quay. Minutes pass, and nothing happens. The Minister's initial flurry of grandiloquent gestures now has been repeated twice, with grins all around. Twenty minutes pass, and still nothing happens: the sea has confounded the divers' efforts to secure the chain to whatever is below. The Minister's grin abates, his gestures become less expansive. He has run out of things to say, and even the sea must not keep a Minister waiting. He and his retinue turn around and abruptly leave.

In the crowd there is speculation as to whether or not anything can be rescued today from such a sea. Another hour passes, the sea's turbulence increases. Nevertheless, an enormous, empty white bladder of limp plastic is floated on the sea near the divers and the chain. Two divers descend with it. A few more minutes pass, and the bladder – now inflated with compressed air – rises to the surface and reveals itself to be a huge balloon. The Minister and his retinue hastily return. The winch chain is now apparently attached to something down

October 4th 1995: the first piece emerges from the water and is placed in front of the Egyptian officials, not helped by the wind and conditions at sea.

below, something which the balloon is helping to raise. The pitch of the barge makes the chain go slack and then lethally snap about. Still, something is on that chain, something massive is resisting its pull. The divers – Empereur among them, identifiable by his white cap, tank, and gloves – gesture and shout to one another and to those on the barge. There is a murmur in the crowd. The hundred or so assembled seem convinced that, whatever the submerged object may be, its resistance – like that of a great marlin after a lengthy battle – is about to be overcome. With each pitch of the barge, the object on the chain approaches the surface and recedes.

No one on shore seems to know what it can be. The divers guide it with ginger assurance, then draw back as it sways too close. Whatever it is, it is very heavy, its inertia is not to be trifled with. The divers again approach their prey, one of them signals to the winch. They again draw back, and the chain pulls taut. One can sense the tension in it as a huge stone object breaks the surface. But the barge pitches forward, and the chain again goes slack. The figure disappears. The barge regains its equilibrium, and the chain once more tightens. The sea begins to withhold its buoyancy, and the chain remains taut. Something is emerging.

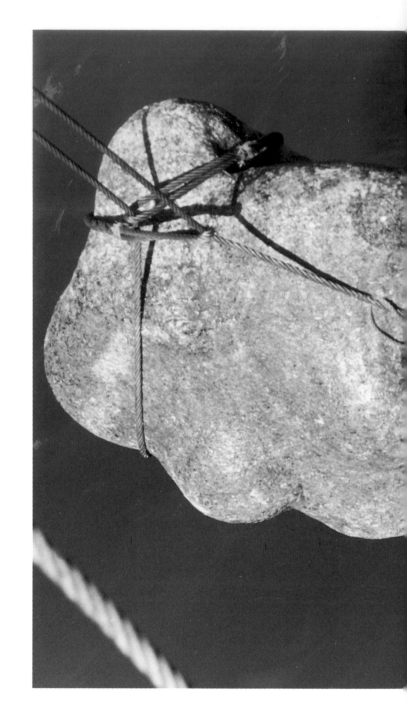

Those on shore see first a place where the stone is broken – a neck from which the head long ago snapped off. Sleek shoulders, massive and rounded, follow the neck out of the water, and the cables descending from the chain have bound them. Another murmur in the crowd, and then a large, collective gasp: below the

This first piece is of a Ptolemaic queen, bearing the traits of a goddess, most probably Isis.

shoulders the heroic, glistening breasts of a powerful goddess, or queen, or goddess queen. Her rib cage then appears, below which the stone again has broken away. But her entire torso has emerged intact. The gasp in the crowd turns to a reverent moan, and then shouts and an outburst of applause.

A Greek man on the quay, impressed by the figure's magnificent breasts, watches them turn in the air as she sways at the end of her tether. With grave authority, he speaks the single word, 'Megalomastia'. His neighbours do not respond, mesmerised and awe-inspired by the forceful beauty of the torso suspended before them. He repeats the word, with emphasis this time, as though they had not heard. 'Megalomastia. These large-breasted sculptures are a category of

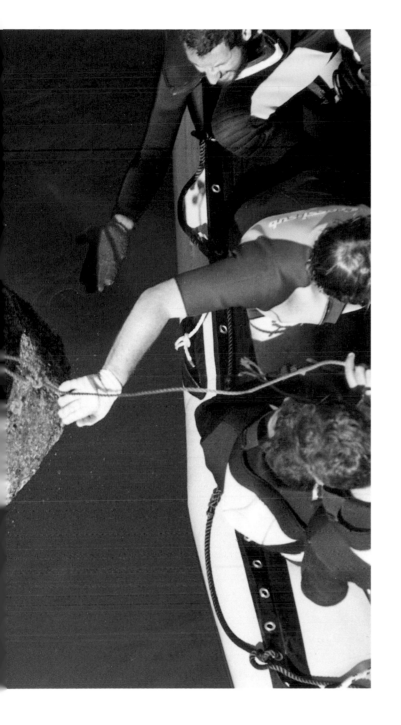

their own. Goddesses among whose principal characteristics is fertility.' The people near him still do not respond to his questionable reduction of what they have before their eyes. Be she Isis, or Aphrodite, or a Ptolemaic queen, she is now weightless above her shattered reflection on the sea. She glistens in the sun with water and with an ageless sensuality, mesmerising the crowd as she must have done to many crowds before them. Beauty is the instant when blending light and form escape from domineering argument, the poet Maxwell Bodenheim once wrote. Jean-Yves Empereur and his team, against severe odds, have brought forth not just evidence of their ability to retrieve shards of a noble culture, they have brought forth also just such an 'instant', and in doing so they have granted all present that day an intimate communion with that ageless sensuality, with the achievement of an artist dead more than two thousand years. For those who were present, the civilization of Hellenism can never again be remote.

On October 4, 1995, Empereur produced a first Alexandrian proof in his long, arduous, magisterial demonstration of, among so much else, Ezra Pound's resonant dictum: 'All ages are contemporaneous.'

JEAN-YVES EMPEREUR
AND THE RETRIEVAL
OF A CULTURE

Assumption of The Risk of Alexandria

D r Empereur and his team have assumed the risk of Alexandria. This is a place of incomparable archaeological riches, minimally explored. To Empereur's colleagues in classical archaeology, it had seemed too Egyptian to bother with; to Egyptologists, too Greek. To property developers over the last two centuries, its surface was potentially too profitable to leave to the archaeologists, regardless of their specialties. Today, Alexandria is an Arab city, to be sure. President Nasser began to disperse the non-Egyptian populations after taking power in the early 1950s, and the ancient principle of ecumenical hospitality, which had assured the greatness also of Arab Spain and the early Ottoman Empire, was replaced by a strident nationalism. Nasser was a leader of the group of Non-Aligned Nations, which preferred not to participate in the frenetic contentions between the US and the USSR The group anointed itself a 'bloc' at Bandung, Burma, in 1955. The following year, the Egyptian seizure of the Suez Canal alerted the world to the fact that Egypt's long submission to the dominance of European influence in its society and culture was drawing to a close -- more

*Jean-Yves Empereur in front of
the Alexandria corniche.*

The land dig of the Diana theatre in Alexandria during the summer of 1994. In front of a mosaic of the Medusa, Jean-Yves Empereur (on the left) and two searchers: Louis Bochaton (middle), Isik Sahin (on the right).

rapidly than most had thought. That European influence, which persists in the architecture of the Corniche and the commercial centre, of the Greco-Roman Museum and the handsome residential quarters such as Shalalat, was a principal component of the cosmopolitanism which for two thousand three hundred years was Alexandria's brilliant appeal. It is a most beguiling city still, although, as the English archaeologist and diver Honor Frost – who figures so prominently in this story – is wont to say, 'It needs a coat of paint.'

'When I dive each morning,' Empereur has said of the sea off Fort Quayt Bey, 'I cannot help but marvel at the importance of this site.' There is never a hint, in his discourse, that he has had a moment's remorse at having assumed the risk of Alexandria. He obtained his teaching diploma – his *aggrégation* – in classical literature, his *doctorat* in archaeology. Through intelligence and application, the standard forms of advancement became available to him, often at a precocious age. In his twelve years at the French School of Archaeology at Athens – with forays to digs also in Turkey and Cyprus – he distinguished himself so brilliantly that, in the words of one colleague, 'the directorship would have been his, had he wanted it.' But he did not want it.

With a boldness that surprised many, he chose instead to create the *Centre d'Études*

Alexandrines – the Centre for Alexandrian Studies – on the seventh floor of a nondescript building near Alexandria's huge soccer stadium. It is there, in two apartments which bracket a landing where a temperamental elevator occasionally deigns to stop, that Jean-Yves Empereur and his French and Egyptian colleagues plan their campaigns, create, on computer, their maps of archaeological sites, and analyze their results. The ambience is much more that of a residence – simultaneously modest, welcoming, and casual – than it is that of an institution which is altering our fundamental perceptions of both underwater archaeology and what was, for three hundred years, the principal civilization of the Western World. Archaeologists, topographers, oceanographers, architects, photographers, filmmakers, writers, government officials come and go, in these quarters, with an informality that removes all inhibition from the exchange of information and ideas. And yet there is a sense, in these rooms, of participation in an enterprise which is larger in scope, in duration, in ultimate

Jean-Yves Empereur on the same dig at the Diana theatre with, on the right, Dominique Allios.

significance than any one person, or any one lifetime. The philosopher of history Ibn Khaldun observed, in the fourteenth century, that a small group of closely connected people, when their shared faith is passionately held, can prevail over the most staggering opposition, can alter policies so long established that they appear immutable. He was writing of the phenomenon of austere tribal societies, at the centre of the lives of which one finds the white flame of religion, of how so often, across the millennia, they have overcome great, bureaucratic governments, the spiritual mission of which has been eroded by expediency and luxury. If the Centre for Alexandrian Studies succeeds in its mission, it will be because of this unity, this dedication, this unanimous faith in a vision shared. The opponent of that mission is, however, nothing as obvious as a corrupt government such as Ibn Khaldun's tribal warriors would have opposed. This opponent is multiple and diffuse. It resides – as so often in the modern world – in the mentality of a

Top: at work in the library of the Centre for Alexandrian Studies, working on documents concerning the lighthouse. In the foreground on the right is Isik Sahin, standing at the centre Mohamed Mustafa, on the left, sitting, Dominique Allios.
Bottom: Jean-Pierre Corteggiani, archaeologist at the French Institute of Oriental Archaeology (IFAO), with Mohamed Mustafa in the background.
Facing page: The body of the colossal statue of Ptolemy as Pharoah. Two divers place the slings of the crane around the statue's torso prior to removing it from the water.

citizenry most of whom are preoccupied, of necessity, with economic survival.

The surface ease that pervades the environment at the Centre overlays an intensity of absolute commitment to the work itself. The historian Mustafa el-Abbadi has written of the Museion as the 'think tank' of Ancient Alexandria – a sort of proto-university to which the Ptolemies attracted the greatest minds of the Hellenistic World. Inspired by Aristotle's Lyceum and Plato's Academy, it was a place where pursuits favored by the Muses – literature, philosophy, science – might be pursued in tranquillity. To another historian, Peter Green, it was a 'research centre', a place, like All Souls at Oxford or the Institute for Advanced Study at Princeton, where the imposed administrative structure was minimal. It was a place where commitment to the creation of new knowledge – and, to a lesser degree, the conveying of knowledge from one generation to the next – was all that ultimately mattered. The Museion, like the great Library of Alexandria, was founded in 297 BCE. The Centre bears similarities to this model, even if much more modest in scale. There is, however, in the case of the Centre, also an additional – an unspoken – dimension to the enterprise. That is the dimension of transcendent obligation, for the new knowledge the Centre is creating is of something integral that was lost, something great and inimitable, a part of our collective consciousness that has sunk beneath the sea.

In the winters since the Centre's founding in 1990, Empereur and his team have excavated sites on land, and preference is given to sites within Alexandria. During the summers, they have explored sites beneath the sea. 'An undersea ruin is different to the extent that it's the archaeologists themselves who dive, there are no archaeological labourers,' as on a land-based dig. 'One therefore sees the excavation differently. We're together eighteen hours out of twenty-

Pages 26-27: At the end of October 1995, a colossal 11.4 ton statue, one of the most impressive of the dig, is lifted from the water by the floating crane.

fours, we have an intense group life — sometimes constraining, but it can go very well, it can be very enriching. This has been the case for the [last several months]. We breakfast together, we lunch, dine, and pass the day together, we pass the evenings together. It's completely different from a land-based dig, where, when it's time to close the work site for the night, one is free to do something else.' The team for an undersea dig can grow to forty or fifty people. 'It's therefore necessary to know how to live together on a daily basis, to work together, to discuss all our problems together. If not, the group stops, it can become paralysed by a little grain of sand. There's a psychological phenomenon to be managed in this, and it's extremely interesting because it brings a completely different human dimension to the excavation...' The model here is, again, more that of Ibn Khaldun's close-knit tribe than of Mustafa el-Abbadi's Museion. One may conclude that the Centre presents a conflation of these two models, and, in doing so, takes on its own, unique identity.

Before living in Greece, Empereur had spent two years in Egypt. 'I began working in Alexandria now twenty years ago.' During his Greek period, he spent a month or two each year in Alexandria. 'I was astonished by the difference between our literary knowledge of Alexandria — we are all the heirs of Alexandria's literature, architecture, medicine, indeed every manner of Alexandrian science and technology — and our complete

ignorance of Alexandrian archaeology. This was somewhat the motivation from the beginning, to see if we could get to know Alexandria a little better by undertaking rescue digs in the heart of the city. The centre of town is currently being renovated, and so the opportunity exists to verify *in situ* what one may hope to discover with these rescue digs.' Alexandria, from its early days in the three hundred years Before the Common Era, was the largest and most important city of the Hellenistic world. 'Any of the other cities of Greece or of the Coast of Asia Minor represented at most one of the quarters of Alexandria.' Empereur goes on, 'The

only city with which one can compare it is the Rome of the Third or Fourth Century [of the Common Era], at the time of its greatest expansion.' This Alexandria represented a 'microcosm where one finds all the peoples of the earth and all the products of the earth, with fabulous riches derived from commerce between India and Egypt. One could find everything in Alexandria.'

And one might argue that Empereur and his associates also, through the interdisciplinary intensity of archaeological inquiry, are finding 'everything in Alexandria.'

Part of the team preparing to dive, during the autumn 1995 campaign. On the right, Jean-Yves Empereur, in the centre Jean Curnier, sitting are Véronique François and Annik Chele, standing behind are Mohamed el-Sayed, Mohammed Mustafa and Alain Peton.

29

Pilgrimage To The Centre

The battle of Issus, circa 333 BC. During the course of this battle Alexander the Great defeated Darius III, King of Persia. Mosaic dating to the 1st century BC, in the National Archaeological Museum of Naples.

The origin of the city which Empereur has engaged was both practical and divine. Homer appeared in a dream to Alexander the Great, instructing him to build a great city which he would name after himself. In the end, it was but one of thirty-two 'Alexandrias' which he created in Europe, Asia, and Africa. But this 'Alexandrea ad Aegyptum', as the Romans later called it, became by far the largest and most powerful, by far the most resonant ot Alexandrias. The young conqueror — he was then only twenty-three — was seen as a liberator

by the Egyptians, for his rule replaced what had been a harsh occupation by the Persians. He was principal among the models Virgil had in mind when fashioning his Aeneas, founder of Rome. He was among the examples Ibn Khaldun had before him when affirming that every new society must be built on a strong religious base. Alexander appears to have known this intuitively, for he made the long, arduous, even dangerous pilgrimage through the Libyan Desert to the Oasis of Siwa, still remote today. There, he consulted the oracle, rendered his obeisance at the Temple of Amun, King of the Egyptian gods. The priests of Amun at Siwa, moved by this act of submission by the supreme warrior of the known world, proclaimed him the Divine Son of Amun and created him a god. From that moment forward, as he approached that place that would become his city, the Greek and Egyptian merged within him, the temporal and divine composed within his skull. He saw himself no longer as the leader of Macedonians or of Greeks alone, he saw himself as the divine leader of all of humankind. 'He was the pioneer', W.W. Tarn has written, 'of one of the supreme revolutions in world outlook, the first man known to us who contemplated the brotherhood of man or the unity of mankind.' It was therefore essential that the city he was creating should encompass, within the concept of Hellenism, all that was human in experience and knowledge. His horse's hooves raised dust clouds as he finally crossed the straight chalk lines with which his architect, Dinocrates, was already laying out the broad streets of what would become Alexandria: the God was entering His City, which He would not live to see.

Left: Detail of the mosaic: portrait of Alexander the Great.

Right: Fishing boats in the port at Alexandria.

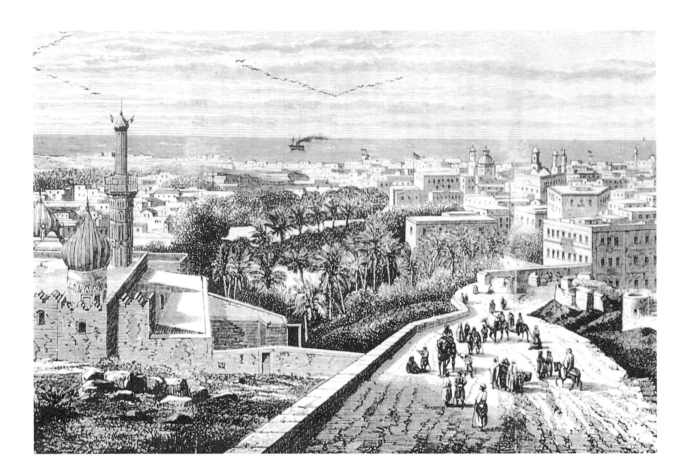

Architecture As The World Again

Alexander died in Babylon, in 323, at the age of thirty-two. One of his Macedonian generals, Ptolemy, inherited the rule of Egypt and advanced construction of the capital at Alexandria. The mentor of the architect Dinocrates had been Hippodamus, who, Aristotle tells us, was a showy eccentric who 'led a very peculiar life', but who created city plans of great clarity and order. Most notably the plans of Piraeus and Miletus, the latter of which, to this day, instructs the designers of cities with its rectangular grid of uncompromising logic. The great philosopher contends that Hippodamus came to this form of organization through a consideration of societal structure. Aristotle – who had been Alexander's tutor – tells us that Hippodamus divided the population into three classes:

> …One of artisans, one of farmers, and the third those who would fight for the state in case of war and bear arms. The land too he divided into three parts: sacred, public and private; sacred land where the customary offerings to the gods could be made, public land that would sustain the military, and private land for farmers.

It was just such a Hippodamian grid which Dinocrates imposed on the coast beside the

twin natural harbours which made Alexandria possible as a great commercial centre. However, the ambition of Alexander and Dinocrates for their city was much larger than that of Hippodamus – the latter saw ten thousand as a city's ideal population. Alexandria's grew to 300,000 in ancient times, some say to 1,000,000. Like Manhattan, it filled its grid – and its grid was then extended to receive still further growth. Differences from the Hippodamian model existed, to be sure, not only in the magnitude and diversity of population, but also in the variety of great institutions which Alexandria, and Manhattan, were conceived to accommodate. Differences existed also in the exhilarating grandeur of Manhattan in the vertical and Alexandria in the horizontal dimension:

Jean-Pierre Corteggiani removing the scrolled capital.

Following pages: Heap of columns in the depths of the underwater archaeological site, with Alessandro Sturla, Stéphane Compoint's assistant.

The first thing one noticed in entering Alexandria by the Gate of the Sun was the beauty of the city. A range of columns went from one end of it to the other. Advancing down them, I came in time to the place that bears the name of Alexander, and there could see the other half of the town, which was equally beautiful. For just as the colonnades stretched ahead of me, so did other colonnades now appear at right angles to them.

–Achilles Tatius, 5th Century C.E.

The 'microcosm' of which Jean-Yves Empereur has spoken was abundantly inclusive. The very neutrality of that grid is the source of its flexibility, the reason that it has welcomed with such ease the constantly changing populations of two thousand three hundred

Facing page: Aerial view of Fort Quayt Bay with Alexandria in the background. The fort was constructed at the end of the 15th century in place of the lighthouse.

The corniche of Alexandria's east port in the setting sun.

years. Little is left of the minor streets Dinocrates laid out, but the course of the great avenues still imparts to the modern city the rudiments of its ancient skeleton, the divisions of its body into the principal quarters. The functions of the three divisions of the concept of Hippodamus altered at Alexandria, but the concept itself held: the north-east quarter became that of the Jews; the western quarter was occupied chiefly by Egyptians – and took its name from the fishing village, Rachotis, which had existed before Alexander's arrival; the most magnificent part of the city was the Royal or Greek quarter, which extended southward from the Eastern Harbour and was called Brucheum. With the advent of the Romans, an official quarter was appended to Brucheum, expanding the city to four *regiones*. The intersection of which Achilles Tatius was writing – and where the 'Sema' (Mausoleum) of Alexander once stood – was that of the east-west Canopic Way (the current Sharia Horeyya) and the north-south Street of the Sema (now the Sharia Nebi Danyal): The clarity of these axes, of this crossing of coordinates, persists over twenty-three centuries in the city that welcomed, in its first two hundred years, the geometer Euclid, the cosmologist Aristarchus, and the global geographer Eratosthenes.

In the computer room of the Centre for Alexandrian Studies, the topographer Xavier Ablain and the archaeologist Christophe Regni call up on the monitor their analytical reconstruction of the engineer Muhammed el-Falaky's own reconstruction of Dinocrates' plan. In 1866, el-Falaky had completed a survey of the modern city in which, knowing the principal axes of Dinocrates' plan, he had chosen a number of points at which to dig down to the ancient

walls and streets. Once he had verified several of these locations, he interpolated on the locations of other streets, including that of the Heptastadeion, the ancient stone causeway which had led, and, widened now to an isthmus, still leads from the mainland across to the island called Pharos. The resulting plan

governed for over a century our perception of Alexandria's original organization. The team at the Centre has determined, through its own manipulation of a wide array of factors affecting the disposition of the Euclidean co-ordinates of Dinocrates' plan, that the brilliance of el-Falaky's reconstruction is not without a flaw – or, rather, that its brilliance consists, in part, precisely in that flaw: the Centre hypothesises that the orientation of his plan is just enough off that of Dinocrates' that it renders all exploratory borings based upon his drawing, as published, to be confusing, at best.

In rectifying the orientation of el-Falaky's plan, the Centre suspects that it has been able to demonstrate that the orientation of the Heptastadeion was integral to the conception of Dinocrates, that it was a direct extension of one of the axes of his plan. The causeway's course across the water, effecting the connection of Pharos to the mainland, extended the physical limits of the plan northward, far beyond the water's edge, until not only the island but the two harbours it separated became visibly a part of the conception of the city.

There is, then, a second great innovation in the plan of Dinocrates, one which altered the world view of Egypt as profoundly as that of Alexander had altered during the pilgrimage to Siwa. At the founding of Alexandria, Egypt already had been, for 2,800 years, a nation which oriented its thinking primarily inward, toward the river which was – geographically, agriculturally, politically, symbolically – (as the Egyptologist Georges Sarkassian pointed out, one late afternoon, in the library of the Centre for Alexandrian Studies) the very source of its life. T.S. Eliot wrote, in *Four Quartets*, of the Mississippi, 'I do not know much about gods; but

Left: Jean-Yves Empereur scrutinizing a votive foot from the temple of Ras al-Soda, which dates from the 2nd century AD and was rebuilt in the centre of Alexandria.

Following pages: A band carved at the base of the sphynx of Psamtik II (XXVI dynasty).

View of ancient Alexandria. The city's location between the desert and the sea is illustrated here, reconstructed by Jean-Claude Golvin. In the foreground is the island of Pharos and the lighthouse.

I think that the river/ is a strong brown god...' With the founding of Alexandria, the global vision of the founder took physical form in a city plan, even as that vision became the policy of the nation: Egypt turned its gaze from the Nile and began also to look outward: it began more than two millennia of engagement with the sea.

Nostalgia For The Infinite

This engagement with the sea itself, and with the lands beyond it and the sky above it, permitted the first kings of the Ptolemaic Dynasty to identify the great minds of the age and then to entice them to their city. Alexandria became known as a place where the boldest intellectual inquiry was both encouraged and subsidised. Jean-Yves Empereur's Centre for Alexandrian Studies resumes, as we have seen, an ancient imperative.

The Museion ('House of the Muses') was much more of a research university than a museum. The Library grew to 700,000 volumes and was the greatest in the world. Ibn Khaldun contends that an emphasis on learning characterises the third phase in the development of a society. The first phase is nomadic; the second is characterised by a settled form of agriculture, and of production and trade within an urban context. Under the early Ptolemies, Alexandria moved into this third phase.

Little is known of Aristarchus of Samos, except that he was born on Samos, that he appears to have worked in Alexandria, that he occasionally is confused with the grammarian Aristarchus of Samothrace, and that he was one of the great geniuses of the Ancient World. Aristarchus was invited to Alexandria by Ptolemy I Soter. There he posited both a sun-centred course for the earth's revolution, which was dismissed by lesser minds as 'impious' (later to be Gallileo's offense also), and a size for the universe which extended so far beyond previous imagining that it became equally inconvenient to entertain. The world of science therefore chose not to embrace that inconvenience, to entertain his assertions, until the age of Nicolaus Copernicus, at the beginning of the sixteenth century of the Common Era. 'Had the world listened,' Timothy Ferris wrote, 'we today would speak of an Aristarchan rather than a Copernican revolution in science, and cosmology might have been spared a millennium of delusion.' Copernicus himself excised from his text mention of the theory of Aristarchus, preferring not to dilute with historic truth the glory of his own achievement. Still, the millennium of delusion, too, was an Alexandrian invention – or, rather, an extended ramble down the blind alley which proceeded from Clodius Ptolemy's comforting re-formulation, in Alexandria, of the old idea of an earth-centred universe.

The presence in Egypt of the greatest of geometers, Euclid, established at the centre of mathematical thinking those pure geometrical principles which Aristarchus, Eratosthenes and others employed as a starting point for their audacious theories in astronomy and geography. Eratosthenes was mathematician, geographer, astronomer, and philosopher. He employed Euclid's method of co-ordinates deriving from axes intersecting at right angles not merely to incorporate the elements of a city – as had Hippodamus and Dinocrates – into a system susceptible to prediction and to measure, but to incorporate the entire globe. One may claim, therefore, an Alexandrian origin for the concept of longitude and latitude, and for an accurate measure of the circumference of the earth. This latter achievement of Eratosthenes was effected by knowing (1) the distance from Alexandria to Aswan, (2) the fact that, on a certain day of the year, at noon, the sun at Aswan casts no shadow, and (3) the length of that shadow in Alexandria at noon of the same day. With this information, Eratosthenes projected a

The lower part of a colossal statue, being cleaned by two divers.

Partial view of the underwater archaeological site.

circumference of 25,000 miles — astonishingly close to what we today know it to be.

At the Centre for Alexandrian Studies, Xavier Ablain and Christophe Regni are computerizing Aristarchus and Eratosthenes. Employing the Global Positioning System (G.P.S.), they compile and analyze information from orbiting satellites, sonar readings taken from ships, existing cartographic data employing the coordinates of longitude and latitude, and sophisticated methods of triangulation to chart the location of submerged sculptures and architectural pieces. They are resuming the charge of their great forebears in the discipline, they are advancing the development and application of the most ancient Alexandrian science into the twenty-first century. And, in a sublime and felicitous irony, they are doing this to rescue the very civilization which gave them the knowledge to do so.

In a further irony, they are employing knowledge created in the Museion and conserved in the Library to salvage the third of Alexandria's pre-eminent achievements, the Pharos.

Sostratos of Cnidus designed and built the great lighthouse of Alexandria, under the sponsorship of Ptolemy II Philadelphus, after the death of his father, Ptolemy I Soter, who had initiated the project, and of his mother, Berenice. The word 'soter' means 'saviour', and, the Egyptologist Jean-Pierre Corteggiani contends that the dedication (known from literary sources; the inscription has not been found) most probably does not refer to those 'two obscure gods, Castor and Pollux, protectors of sailors'. The Pharos was completed around 285 Before the Common Era. The writer Hala Halim has written extensively of Alexandria and the activities of the Centre for Alexandrian Studies. Among the accounts of the lighthouse she has collected, one of the most famous is that of the ancient geographer, Strabo:

> *Pharos is a small oblong island, and lies quite close to the continent…This extremity itself of the island is a rock, washed by the sea on all sides, with a tower upon it of the same name as the island, admirably constructed of white marble [more likely granite], with several storeys.*

In his book, *The Sacred and the Profane*, the historian of religion Mircea Eliade writes, of the Aboriginal Achilpa people of Australia, that, after walking all day through the desert, they force the sharpened point of a long wooden stake they carry with them into the ground to mark the place where they will stop for the night. They see the stake as the precise centre of their world, as the axis of the earth. The lighthouse which Sostratos built on the island of Pharos became the centre and axis of the all-encompassing world of Hellenism envisaged by Alexander. Dinocrates had extended the city across the water by means of the Heptastadeion and, as we have noted, claimed the island of Pharos and the two harbours it separated as — conceptually and perceptually — part of Alexandria. Sostratos now took the horizontal axis represented by the Heptastadeion and turned it ninety degrees, upward into the air, engaging the third dimension in the Euclidean system of coordinates: X, Y, and now Z. He did so not with a solid obelisk but with a hollow tower. He complemented Dinocrates' plan by creating a master demonstration of the principle that made Manhattan possible: he turned the grid on its edge to invite the human habitation of the sky. He created the first skyscraper.

Among the accounts of the lighthouse itself which Halim has compiled, here is that of Ibn Jubair, a traveller at the time of the Crusades:

> *One of the most magnificent of what we have seen of Alexandria's wonders is the lighthouse which God the Almighty and Sublime has led His servants to construct as a wonder in the beholder and a guide to the voyager, without which he would never reach the shores of Alexandria. [From the sea] you can see it from a distance of seventy miles from the city… From within, it is very spacious with many corridors, entrances and rooms to the extent that one can easily lose one's way inside it… Atop it is a mosque said to be blessed where people pray to obtain benediction… We prayed in the aforementioned blessed mosque and saw the wonders of its construction to which no description can do justice.*

Following pages: One of the blocks from the door post of the lighthouse being removed from the water at the end of October 1995.

47

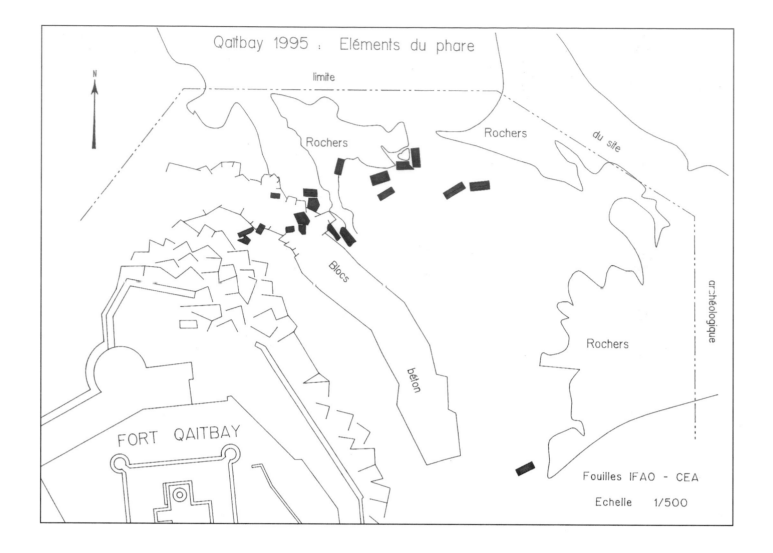

Qaïtbay 1995 : Eléments du phare

limite

Rochers

Rochers

du site

archéologique

Blocs

béton

Rochers

FORT QAITBAY

Fouilles IFAO - CEA

Echelle   1/500

Two maps of the site being established by the team during their pin-pointing dives. The top map shows the alignment of the remains of the lighthouse, weighing more than 20 tons, shown here in red. These monumental pieces are partly caught beneath huge concrete blocks installed to protect the port from storms.

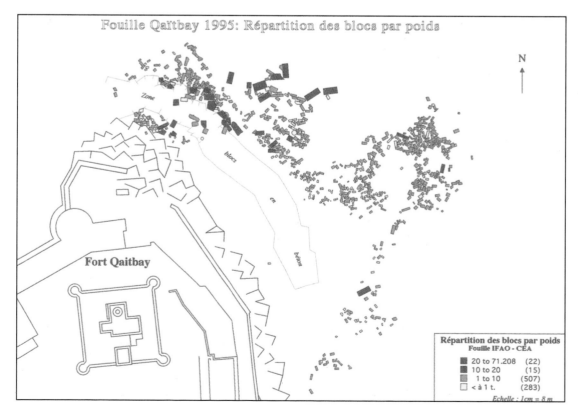

Fouille Qaïtbay 1995: Répartition des blocs par poids

N

Zone

blocs

en

béton

Fort Qaïtbay

Répartition des blocs par poids
Fouille IFAO - CEA

- 20 to 71.208   (22)
- 10 to 20   (15)
- 1 to 10   (507)
- < à 1 t.   (283)

Echelle : 1cm = 8 m

How natural – perhaps inevitable – that the very summit of the only secular Wonder of the Ancient World should, through its awesome grandeur, invite appropriation for religious use, for a mosque. Is it possible that this mosque was the origin of the contention that the Pharos, with its square base, octagonal mid-section, and cylindrical upper storey was the model for the design of minarets? The word 'minaret' itself appears to be descended from the Arabic word for the Pharos, 'el Manarah', which appears in the Koran. Yet how, one must wonder, did the mosque and the great beacon fire of the Pharos co-exist so high above the earth?

If the lighthouse which took the name of the island on which it stood, Pharos, was the Empire State Building of the Ancient World, it was also the Statue of Liberty – which, few recognise, is itself a lighthouse. The fire at the summit of the Pharos, sustained by wood hauled up a great interior ramp, projected – with the aid of a huge mirror designed, some contend, by the mathematician Archimedes – the visual precinct of the city seventy miles through the night, across a most devious sea. Strabo tells us, in his *Geography*, that the Coast of Egypt was notorious for the submerged sand bar, a graveyard for ships, which continued eastward from Libya all along the Egyptian Coast, and from which the harbours of Alexandria provided the principal – and almost the only – haven. The Pharos was a beacon to all travellers, an unassailable physical proof of the pre-eminence of Alexandria, a sign of hope to those of all nations who were 'yearning to breathe free' in the heady, cosmopolitan air of Hellenism. It was the still point of the turning world, the ever-fixèd mark that looks upon tempests and is never shaken.

Well, almost never. The Pharos did stand for 700 years, before its incremental submission to those earthquakes that consigned it, its sculptures, various palaces and temples, and myriad other monuments to the sea floor. Halim retrieves, for our contemplation, the poignant immediacy of Ibn Battuta's account of the building:

> At length on April 5th (1326) we reached Alexandria…I went to see the lighthouse on this occasion and found one of its faces in ruins. It is a very high square building, and its door is above the level of the earth. Opposite the door, and of the same height, is a building from which there is a plank bridge to the door; if this is removed there is no means of entrance…It is situated on a high mound and lies three miles from the city on a long tongue of land which juts out into the sea from close by the city wall, so that the lighthouse cannot be reached by land except from the city. On my return to the West in the year 750 [1349] I visited the lighthouse again, and found that it had fallen into so ruinous a condition that it was not possible to enter it. Al-Malik an-Nasir had started to build a similar lighthouse alongside it but was prevented by death from completing the work.

But even then the influence of Pharos continued. It is quite likely that it became the starting point for the design of innumerable lighthouses, minarets, and bell towers across the ages — even, possibly (for images of it were present in places where architecture was taught), for numerous skyscrapers of the late nineteenth and early twentieth centuries. But, then, just as possibly, the widely-known 1909 reconstructive drawing by Hermann Thiersch, published in his book, *Pharos: Antike Islam und Occident*, reflects, for its time, the reigning imagery in the West of the design of the tall building. Corteggiani concludes that Thiersch's drawing, 'with its decorations and undulating cornices at each level,' shall seem, once the evidence of the current project has sufficiently accrumulated, ' truly fanciful, from here on out'. We have records, after all, that to Chinese travellers the Pharos appeared to be a tall 'pagoda'.

Jean-Yves Empereur recalls his own impressions on first diving at this site:

Watercolour by Yousef Shoukry, showing the lighthouse based on the reconstruction of Hermann Thiersch. Visible is the square foundation, followed by the octagonal body topped by a small tower and finished with a statue of Zeus. (Private collection of Jean-Yves Empereur.)

> At first glance, the chaos was incomprehensible. There were elements of Pharaonic history and others which had been part of Greek monuments. We quickly elaborated several hypotheses. One took into account the collapse of the Pharos. These huge blocks were disposed as though they had fallen in a line, and yet they are so imposing that they could have belonged only to a monumental edifice, and certain pieces resemble parts of corners or parapets, such as the Pharos would have incorporated. So...

He invites his listeners to draw their own conclusions.

The Egyptologist Jean-Pierre Coteggiani suggests, further, that the findings of Empereur's team mean that:

> Perhaps it's necessary to begin to imagine that the Pharos was a little less Greek and a little more Egyptian than the specialist had thought up until today. Architects of the Hellenistic era already had a taste for Egyptian marvels. We can suppose that they made two sorts of re-use of them. A re-use of monuments as decorative elements: obelisks, sphinxes, statues, etc.; a re-use of materials, such as blocks of granite from Aswan. It appears that Pharaonic monuments existed in Alexandria, and this we never imagined.

The monuments of Pharaonic provenance which have been found to date were transported to Alexandria from distant, more ancient sites, such as Heliopolis, near what is now Cairo. And yet some idea of an Alexandrian architectural style resides in the archtectural remnants of the Ptolemaic age.

So celebrated was the Pharos that it has pervaded the languages of the world. Variations

Map of ancient Alexandria by the astronomer Mahmoud el-Falaki, made in 1866. (Private collection of Jean-Yves Empereur.)

of the word 'Pharos' have taken on the meaning 'lighthouse' in many languages. Moreover, the word used for an automobile headlight in Paris and Martinique and Tahiti derives from it ('phare'), in Milan ('faro') and Barcelona and Santiago de Chile (also 'faro'). It is echoed in the name of a city of the Portuguese coast ('Faro'), and it has lent its cachet to the word for the 'science of lighthouses' ('pharology').

Homer tells us that the word 'Pharos' came into Greece with Menalaus, after he and Helen stopped at the little island on their (circuitous) way home from Troy:

> *I was in Egypt – longing to make for home but still kept lingering by the gods because I had failed to offer them acceptable hecatombs. Now, away from the shore, in the wash of waves, there lies an island that men call Pharos… In this place the gods kept me for twenty days.*

One surmise is that the word 'Pharos' is a corruption of 'Pharaoh', which itself means 'great house'. If so, the island certainly grew into its name with the construction of the towering edifice of Sostratos. In fact, when one thinks of the career of Pharos – in so many images and stories and poems across history – as the very emblem of Alexandria, it is enticing to think of the whole of the capital of Hellenism as a single 'great house', and to recall the architect Louis Kahn's memorable phrase, 'The city is an agreement among rooms'. Indeed, Empereur himself has referred to Ancient Alexandria as 'la ville phare du monde méditerranéen', 'the lighthouse city of the Mediterranean World'.

By the year 270 Before the Common Era, the Pharos already had become, in literature, a presence in which Alexandria and the World of Hellenism might feasibly be resumed. The Alexandrian poet Callimachus, so famous for his terse, epigrammatic wit, wrote fulsomely on the death, in that year, of the Egyptian Queen Arsinoë. He places her sister, Philotera, who is already dead, in Greece, from where she looks south:

> …But she, Philotera, noticed the smoke, the indicator of the funeral pyre, which was carried by the breezes as it rolled curling…and along the mid-surface of the Thracian [Aegean] Sea. For a short time ago she had left Sicilian Enna, and was walking on the hills of Lemnos [a Greek island] returning from her visit to Deo [Demeter]. But she knew not of you [i.e., of Arsinoë's death], O stolen by the gods, and said… 'Charis, sit on top of Mount Athos, and see if the fire comes from the…plain…which city has perished, which city all on fire sends forth this light? I am anxious. But fly off…' And she [Charis], when she flew onto the snow-covered peak, which is said to be nearest to the pole-star, and cast her eyes towards the famous [coast] of Pharos, cried out faint at heart…. 'Yes, yes…the smoke is coming from your city [i.e., from Alexandria]…'…Charis said sad words to her: 'Please do not weep for your land – your Pharos has not been burnt – nor for…other evil…your city [is full of] lament…not as though a person of lower rank [were dead?]…but one of the great ones…they are weeping over your one and only sister dead. Wherever you glance the cities of the land are clad in black.' 22

Bust of Serapis, a divinity brought to Egypt by Ptolemy I. Statue dating to the period of the Roman Emperor Hadrian (2nd century AD).

Fifteen years after its construction, the noble and unique lighthouse of Alexandria, Wonder of the Ancient World, was already standing for the great city and the civilization of which it was the capital. And so, we are invited to conclude, the Pharos also rose to that realm where the loftiest earth-anchored presences mingle with the gods and the plenitude of stars. The Pharos, like the great observatories, participated, if only by its sheer height, in the enterprise of astronomy. Its fire, to the most distant ships, took on the aspect and the function of a star, became, to the navigator, an addendum to the calculus of Aristarchus, as he triangulated his ship's course to safety through the treacherous night.

'The God Abandons Antony'

The scientific breakthroughs of Hellenistic civilization were indeed considerable. In the arts and humanities, however, Alexandria was noted more for its accumulation of knowledge created in the past, the refined study of that knowledge, and the transference of that knowledge to succeeding generations, than for astonishing creative breakthroughs in literature, music, architecture, sculpture or painting. In fact, there is a clever epigram of uncertain origin that summarises, without charity, what the world later perceived as Alexandria's particular form of barren excess:

> Egypt has its wild recluses,
> book-bewildered anchorites,
> in the hen coop of the Muses,
> keeping up their endless fights.

Self-indulgence too, then, can be an aspect of think tanks, and of societies which place inordinate emphasis on isolate cerebration, dismissing the value of a collegiality such as that which increases, so abundantly, the intellectual productivity of the Centre for Alexandrian Studies. Einstein, surrounded by the self-importance of some of his colleagues at the Institute for Advanced Study, once said: 'Princeton is a town full of dwarves on stilts'.

Where breakthroughs in the humanities did occur, one may credit an openness to multiple influences, principally – in the case of Alexandria – those resulting from the interpenetration of the Egyptian and the Greek. The energies thus released, especially in architecture, sculpture, and (one suspects, for we can know less of this) painting, produced – as in the cultures of Gandhara, Kushan, and Commagene – a hybrid art of an undeniable, if peculiar, power. The impetus for this hybridization was never purely artistic. In the case of Alexandria, the Founder's insight into the imperative to meld the Greek and Egyptian religions resulted, under the Ptolemies, in the

Jean-Pierre Corteggiani cleaning a block of calcite dating from the reign of Sethi I.

creation of a tutelary god for their kingdom, a combination of the god Osiris and the sacred Apis Bull. Osiris was thought to have ruled Egypt in an ideal time before the founding of the nation, and, indeed, the dead pharaohs were considered to have become embodiments of Osiris. The power and vitality of each Apis Bull affirmed on this earth the authority of each pharaoh's sacred status. The recorded dates of each bull's coronation and death (by drowning, at the hands of priests) correspond to those of the particular pharaoh each bull represented. The convergence, therefore, of the legendary Osiris and the vital Apis Bull in the hybrid deity, Serapis, arrogated to the Ptolemies a double dose of divine legitimacy. Sculptural representations of Serapis run a stylistic gamut from the hirsute Greek gentleman in Alexandria's Greco-Roman Museum to more traditionally Egyptian types who, nonetheless, have been subtly modelled with a classical attention to musculature.

In architecture, one finds the Egyptian emphasis on continuous mass – on unbroken expanses of wall in cut and finished stone – taking precedence, at Alexandria, over the columnar structures of the Greeks, although both modes–and amalgams of the two, as Corteggiani points out – no doubt were in evidence. Alexandria may have been one of the few places where, within the eye's brief compass, one might have seen, in 250 BCE, architectural influences from twenty-eight centuries, those centuries in which, the architect Louis Kahn once said , 'the wall parted and the columns became.' Among the amalgams we may consider is an Alexandrian column capital found beneath the sea at the Pharos site, one which modifies the Ionic precedent of the Greeks to incorporate the papyrus which was the symbol of Lower Egypt. Other capitals combine the papyrus and the lotus, the intertwining of which symbolised the marriage, around 3,100 BCE, of the Upper and Lower kingdoms. (Still others, of later date, also incorporate a cross, evidencing the existence of Coptic Egypt as the oldest Christian nation). The religious and the political were, of course, inseparable in the culture of Alexandria, and their unitary nature, we may conclude, pervaded the visual arts.

In a way, a hybrid art, initially exhilarating, can come to a quick exhaustion, for it is, in the end, a singular conceit: it is a bit like building an entire novel or film around a joke which is essentially a one-liner. For the hybrid not to exhaust the soil in which it is planted, new influences continually must be grafted on, new nutrients mixed with the earth from which it draws its life. And what is new must be of sufficient vitality to engage the passions of the artists who are the agency through which the culture moves (if indeed it shall move) from strength to ever-greater strength.

Similarly, in order to sustain, in the political realm, the marriage of the Greek and Egyptian traditions, there was the need to sustain, as well, the essential fiction of the unified – unifying – divinity of Alexander – of the ascetic, visionary Founder, and of his Mission as Warrior-Ruler.

By the time of Cleopatra and of Antony, this fiction, in spite of its regeneration through Serapis and various deified Ptolemies, had lost its power. The functions of Warrior and Ruler had been terminally split: Cleopatra, the Ruler whose excessive opulence eroded the effectiveness of her superior intelligence, presented a hollow — even vulgar — impersonation of the goddess Isis; Antony, the Warrior whose gifts as a tactician ultimately were outweighed by his limitations as a strategist, became so chronically inebriated with wine and his paramour's much-fabled charms that, by his death and that of his lady in 30 BCE, not only Herakles, his 'forebear' (in the accounts of Shakespeare and his source, Plutarch), abandoned him, but (in Cavafy's formulation) the god who was the city itself, Alexandria.

The literary critic David Quint finds, in Virgil's recounting of the great sea battle of Actium in 31 BCE, in which the forces of Antony and Cleopatra were resoundingly defeated, an opposition of factors not unlike those which Ibn Khaldun identified 1,200 years later as pertaining to conqueror and conquered in the overthrow of kingdoms. The purposeful unity of Rome's forces under Octavian prevails over the cosmopolite diversity of Alexandria's forces under Antony and Cleopatra. That purpose is the continued primacy of the Roman imperium — with its tight-knit (if disputatious) family of Olympian gods — over the ill-conceived adventure of Egyptian secession — with its rag-tag synthesis of Greek and Egyptian deities. (Serapis is not singled out, but Virgil has the dog-head Anubis bark in incomprehensible futility over Alexandria's burning fleet.) The flight of Cleopatra from a secure banlieue of the battle site is, of course, the flight of a civilization rotten from an excess of luxury and languor. In three hundred years, from 331 BCE to 31 BCE, Alexandria had passed from the ascendant through the descendant phase of Ibn Khaldun's prescription.

The subsequent terror of the populace of Alexandria as Octavian's army, now almost unopposed, approached from the east, has not been recorded. It is of little interest to Shakespeare when he has the dramatic deaths of his protagonists to portray. We do, however, have a modern parallel to the plight of those whom Antony's drunken lassitude betrayed. In 1942, Rommel's army of Germans and Italians was approaching from Libya, across the Western Desert. Older residents of Alexandria remember, as though it were yesterday, the terror of the populace at that time. On one of the October days that the first sculptures were being removed from the sea, a Greek woman recounted the panic in the town fifty three years before: 'Rommel seemed unstoppable. The Allies were fleeing the city. The dependents and the diplomats and the other offficial English were departing as quickly as they could. With them, that somber structure of bureaucratic order — which had seemed, at times, eternal, unchanging, and unbearably heavy — was evaporating like spume from a wave, and in the blink of an eye. You can't imagine how terrified we were. My mother and father tried everything to get my sisters and me out. Nothing seemed to work. They tried to keep us calm, but at night we overheard them talking softly to each other, in their desperation, of what might happen to us at the hands of the German soldiers. The fighting was still a hundred kilometres away, and yet quite late on certain nights I was sure I could hear the rumble of the

guns.' Rommel was stopped at Alamein, but Octavian entered the city, which the god was abandoning.

The departure of the god in his several guises may have begun with the dramatic end of the Ptolemaic Dynasty, but it continued for many centuries, as the sculptures and the temples and the great institutions were destroyed or removed – or, as in the case of so many, they fell or were pushed into the sea. By the fourteenth century, when the Pharos was nothing more than a scattering of rubble, few of the sculptures which represented the deities and divine rulers were still in evidence. Aside from those which have found the way to museums, their abandonment of the city was complete. Their long night sea journey had begun, and, with few exceptions, it would continue until the campaigns of the Centre for Alexandrian Studies in the middle of the last decade of the twentieth century.

The head of a woman, usually identified as Cleopatra.

Following pages: This sphynx from the period of Sethi I contacts air for the first time after many centuries of submersion.

CONSERVATORS
OF THE PALIMPSEST

Pal.imp.sest, n., a parchment, tablet, etc. that has been written upon or inscribed two or three times, the previous text or texts having been imperfectly erased and remaining, therefore, still visible.

-Webster's New World Dictionary of the American Language, 1959

In the wake of the Pioneers

The Campaign of 1995, as conceived and executed by the Classical Archaeologist Jean-Yves Empereur, the Egyptologists Jean-Pierre Corteggiani and Georges Sarkassian, and the French-Egyptian team of the Centre for Alexandrian Studies was indeed the beginning of a new phase in the career of Alexandria, both as an arena for archaeological exploration and as a presence of ever-gathering power in the consciousness of world civilization. It was also, however, the culmination of more than three decades of usually lonely struggle by those who were willing to risk their time, their money, and even their lives in order to honour through their witness the majesty of the superimposed layers of a submerged culture, a culture obscured by sand, sewage sludge, and the accumulated detritus of more than a thousand years.

This sphinx, resting on the barge with a papyrus column, is the only, of the dozen retrieved, to have kept its head.

Until the second decade of the Twentieth Century, on those days when the sea was calm, one could look out from the shore and see, at least, beneath the few clouds reflected on the Eastern Harbour's still surface, the foundations of the temples and the palaces of the dynasty of the Ptolemies, of Cleopatra and of Antony. All this had changed by the early 1960s, when Kemal Abu el-Saadat, a diver of great courage, high intelligence, and little formal education descended beneath the sea just beyond the Eastern Harbour and emerged with news of more than those few, suggestive walls, with news of unimaginable cultural riches. He told his remarkable story of colossi and sphinxes and the ruins of whole buildings to the authorities who, unlike this simple man of the sea, were certified to know such things: since Saadat was virtually unlettered, his findings, in the opinion of the specialists, must be nothing but mere fantasy. However, according to Jean-Yves Empereur, Saadat was successful in

Jean-Yves Empereur working on the lifting of a papyrus column.

accomplishing much more than simply alerting the world to the existence of an extraordinary site. 'He succeeded in convincing the Egyptian Navy to retrieve [from the sea bed] an enormous statue of Isis now to be found at [Alexandria's] Maritime Museum.' In so doing, he announced that the long night sea journey of the submerged culture might soon end.

Kemal Abu el-Saadat was not one to be deterred. He persisted until, as Empereur recounts, in 1968, 'the Egyptian Government requested expert assistance from UNESCO', which arrived in the inimitable form of the diminutive, highly articulate, relentlessly determined Honor Frost, 'an archaeologist well-known in the milieu of undersea divers, who arrived with a geological engineer from Paris, and who prepared a little report published in 1974, in which she provided several drawings of the [underwater] site which she had managed to make in spite of quite adverse weather conditions.' Empereur goes on to note, with considerable admiration, that Frost, without the benefit of photography, nonetheless produced both drawings and 'a description sufficiently detailed to give a good idea of the site'.

In fact, Saadat and Frost, together, mapped the seabed and many of its stone treasures using pieces of rope and a method of triangulation which, though primitive in comparison to the highly technological modes of cartography currently employed by the Centre's topologist Xavier Ablain and his archaeologist colleagues, utilises the same ancient Alexandrian knowledge. Euclid and Eratosthenes would find equally familiar – perhaps identical – the principles underlying the 'Ablain method' of sonar, satellites, and computers and the 'Saadat-Frost method' of a cool eye, a concentrated mind, and numerous bits of string. When the hand-made drawing of 1968 was overlain with the computer-generated drawing of 1995, and the lineaments of the two converged, the only regret that mingled with Honor Frost's

Many years after having studied underwater artefacts, the British archaeologist Honor Frost prepares to dive with this new team, on the 4th of October 1995.

Following pages: Before surfacing, Jean-Yves Empereur (in the background) and Pierre Bruno (left) clear sand from a sphinx with the help of a hydraulic vacuum.

triumphant satisfaction was that her courageous partner had not lived to savor this final vindication.

Kemal Abu el-Saadat was killed, in the 1970s, on a dive to salvage the remnant treasures and the fittings of Napoleon's flagship, L'Orient, sunk by the British, in 1798, off the coast at Aboukir. Some of what he found there – coins and objects in silver, terra cotta, glass, and iron – are displayed in the museum of Fort Quayt Bey, on the site of the ancient lighthouse, overlooking the place in the sea where he and Honor Frost had dived, where the Isis Pharia had been plucked from her company of stone gods and goddesses, kings and queens, broken columns and vigilant sphinxes.

It was Napoleon who called upon the French to honour the great culture of Egypt, who established the centres of scholarship and first mounted the great excavations which would bring so much of the Egyptian past so resoundingly into our present consciousness. Walking through the exhibition at Fort Quayt Bey, Honor Frost was visibly moved by the evidence of her friend's last and fatal expedition. The encrusted, corroded, often sea-worn objects from Napoleon's ship became Saadat's mute offering to the French out of their own past, became an emblem of the diver's persistence even from beyond the grave, an exhortation to Napoleon's compatriots to resume, at Alexandria, in partnership with Saadat's own people, the emperor's lapsed imperative.

Finally, two decades after the diver's death, Nicolas Grimal of the Institut Français d'Archéologie Orientale, representatives of the Louvre, of the Fondation Elf, of the Fondation Electricité de France, Stéphane Compoint and the photographers of SYGMA, the filmmakers Andrew Snell, Thierry Ragobert, and Stéphane Millière of Gédéon, have joined with Walid el-Nasri and other divers of the Egyptian Navy, representatives of the Supreme Council of Antiquities, the Greco-Roman Museum and numerous others to support the Centre for Alexandrian Studies in providing an

Left: Some of the dig material under a wooden kiosk near the Quayt Bey Fort.

The head and torso of a colossal Ptolemaic statue of a queen.

answer worthy of the question posed, from beyond the grave, by Kemal Abu el-Saadat.

Asma el-Bakri has been called 'the Cultural Conscience of Egypt'. Not everyone listens to his conscience, but it is very difficult not to listen to Asma el-Bakri. There no doubt have been instances of cultural officials or government ministers suddenly remembering urgent meetings elsewhere, or simply scurrying around street corners, when alerted to the fact that Ms el-Bakri is in the outer office or rising from her table at the café across the square. She has the reputation for being as persistently inconvenient as the truth.

She is also as vigilant as a sphinx and considerably more energetic. 'It was only when Asma el-Bakri, a well-known Egyptian filmmaker whose work has won prizes in France,' Empereur explained, 'wanted to make a film on the [Greco-Roman] Museum of Alexandria which included footage of a number of exterior locations, that provided the occasion [for her] to dive at the [Fort Quayt Bey] site...' The year was 1993.

Asma el-Bakri—filmmaker, cultural conscience, force of nature, descended beneath the waves near the Pharos site and beheld the superimposition of huge, U-shaped blocks of concrete — each weighing several tons — upon the top layer of stone sphinxes, columns, and colossi of the ancient city. The blocks of concrete had been dropped — still were being dropped — by the Government, from a great barge, to create a breakwater which would protect the Eastern Harbour from the actions of the sea. What would protect the submerged stone figures from the actions of the Government had not yet been addressed.

When el-Bakri emerged with her heart-rending footage and heart-stirring anger, a furore arose which

The base of an Ionic column.

increased exponentially her inconvenience rating in the Corridors of Power. She quickly enlisted the help of the influential architect and noted preservationist Muhammed Awad and others in the cause. A veritable masterpiece of bureaucratic 'even-handedness' resulted from the press fuss el-Bakri precipitated, a press fuss which Jean-Pierre Corteggiani, employing an adjective drawn from his archaeological vocabulary, termed 'colossal'. That master-piece, which must have tested even el-Bakri's capacity for rueful irony, authorised both the removal from the sea of several historic sculptures and the continued disposition on the top of those ruins of the ever-proliferating accumulation of huge blocks of concrete.

At the end of October 1995, Jean-Yves Empereur (on the right) and Jean-Pierre Corteggiani examine a colossal Ptolemaic Statue. This first contact with open air allows the calculation of a preliminary dating which is impossible under water.

One did not have to don a wet suit in order to appreciate the wildly contradictory nature of this peculiar 'solution'. One simply needed to observe, from the shore, on any of a number of sunny days in October, 1995, as the large winch barge emerged from the Eastern Harbour and moved, with the inexorable slowness of the bureaucratic 'reasoning' it symbolised, to participate either in a current rescue from the seabed or the impeding of future rescues.

The ironies were not limited to the sea and the sea floor. On land, not only Empereur's team and the ubiquitous Asma el-Bakri were among those alert to and involved in the salvaging of layer upon layer of Alexandria's patrimony. The architect Muhammed Awad, the historian Mustafa el-Abbadi, and the writer Hala Halim are only a few of the others active on multiple fronts. Awad has sought especially to conserve the outstanding examples of Alexandria's nineteenth and twentieth century architecture, including, most recently, even so modest a unique structure as the cottage in which Lawrence Durrell lived during the period depicted in The Alexandria Quartet. Professor el-Abbadi, who has written with a cultivated lucidity about, among so much else, the Museion and Ancient Library, has spoken with persuasive clarity and alarm about another contradictory policy, that by which a large, new library of Alexandria is being constructed on the site of the renowned Ancient Library before the ruins of the ancient structure could be excavated by archaeologists. The loss for at least another century of an archaeological opportunity which existed, however briefly, as self-evidently unique reflects a 'triumph' of expediency over responsibility in planning, a 'triumph' which could – and perhaps will – appear in a text book on urban conservation under the heading, 'What Not To Do'.

Hala Halim's articulate overview of all these issues and personalities sustains them at the level of consciousness of the populace through the pages of Al-Ahram Weekly. Hers is the diary of Alexandria's struggle with itself, of the advances and reverses of the force of culture against that of commerce, of the force of quality against that of quantity, of the force of the city's collective memory against that which would obliterate that memory forever.

Edward Koch, when Mayor of New York, used to ask citizens in the street, 'How'm I doing?' The mayors and governors and ministers, the developers and bureaucrats and civic leaders, the archaeologists and classicists and Egyptologists of her country need not step into the street to find out how they are doing. Hala Halim, with the absolute integrity which is the foundation of her graceful style, will courteously tell them. Her continuing act of witness has a cumulative effectiveness. It is possible that the more farsighted of those about whom she writes now consider what they will be able to say when asked by their grandchildren, 'What did you do to rescue the ancient culture of our city?' Hala Halim, like the great chroniclers of the past, provides the curious of subsequent generations with a way to find out.

The Pharos Campaign of 1995

Jean-Pierre Corteggiani cleaning a fragment from an obelisk dating to Sethi I. This obelisk was originally thought to date from the reign of Ramses II, but after examination was instead determined to originate from his father's era.

Among the most dramatic entries, for 1995, in those feature articles which are Halim's public diary, are those which have addressed the activities of the team Jean-Yves Empereur has assembled for the Pharos Campaign.

After several centuries under water, the pieces need to be desalinated. The sphinx at the top and the colossal statue of Ptolemy will soak for several months in this desalination bath. Mohamed Mansur (left) and Dreck (right) are busy scraping them clean.

On October 4, on the rampart of Fort Quayt Bey, while others in the crowd of journalists, archaeologists, cultural officials, and the curious public awaited, in various states of passivity, the results of the battle of Empereur's rescue team against a recalcitrant sea, Hala Halim conversed with a highly articulate Englishwoman in her seventies. Halim asked the questions, the Englishwoman answered. At length. The polite deference of the inquisitor proved the perfect means by which to elicit both an analysis of the work in progress on the turbulent surface before their eyes, and an informed conjecture as to the probable activity, at each moment, of the divers below the waves. It proved also to be the perfect means by which to elicit an anecdotal history of archaeological diving around the Mediterranean over the last half century. The Englishwoman, of course, was Honor Frost.

As the two women talked, Empereur's undertaking took on, through the words of Honor Frost, an ever-increasing intensity of significance. It was as though the whole, vast history of the cultural exploration of the mother of seas had come down to the present moment, had been prelude to the current enterprise — even as the current enterprise was prelude to the coming years (more likely decades) of exploration, of success and of failure, in this great re-definition of Alexandria as a pivot point in the history of Egypt, in the melding of the Greek and the Egyptian and the Jewish that gave us the framework of Hellenism, and the first world city.

The torso that emerged on October 4, 1995, was, then, both culmination and commencement.

Sandrine Elaigne and Dominique Allios recording the position and size of blocks, columns and statues which rest at the foot of Fort Quayt Bey. In the background is the colossal statue of Ptolemy.

Following pages: The statue of Ptolemy being lifted by Louis Bochaton (left) and Jean Curnier (right). Having wrapped the cable around the blocks, the divers attach balloons which, when filled with compressed air, will allow the blocks to be lifted, despite their weight of several tons. At the surface, the cranes attach to the cables and carry the blocks to land.

*The east port of Alexandria,
viewed from the Eastern side.*

In the subsequent weeks, thirty three other architectural pieces, colossi, and sphinxes followed her out of the sea. That majestic procession was interrupted, repeatedly, by bad weather and the unavailability of the barge. The barge was often needed elsewhere – or, even more exasperatingly, needed in the very same place, but for that disposition of blocks of concrete that impeded the divers' work, damaged the submerged architectural and sculptural pieces, and endangered all who, in the hope of rescuing them, descended beneath the waves.

After days of delays, and in mounting anxiety over the fast-approaching end of the season and expiration of the permit to remove pieces, Empereur and his team arose on the morning of October 10 and noted that the sea had calmed, if only a little. The wind was not accelerating the thrashing of the palm fronds with quite the intensity of the preceding days. Still, their green blades scraped against one another as swiftly as knives in the hands of a sharpener. The barge was promised for that morning – which, however, Empereur well knew,

did not mean that its use would actually be provided. And yet, on this second Tuesday of the month, the morning after the harvest feast of the Jews, a major effort was launched in what long had been the largest city of the Jews, as it had been of the Greeks, and of the Egyptians themselves. The team that would execute this complex and delicate mission began assembling before 8:00 AM near the pavilion in the courtyard of Fort Quayt Bey. Empereur, dressed in hiking shorts and a worn khaki jacket like those favored by journalists entering war zones, was among the first to arrive. Around his neck, the signature incongruity of a silk foulard. He was Graham Greene in Hanoi, Schliemann in Anatolia, Balanchine finally disembarking in New York.

Equipment was brought out from the barrel-vaulted stone chambers that most probably had once been stables. The rough grate of metal air tanks against the paving stones sounded like that of artillery shells being moved into place, or of the armor of generals being prepared before battle – that of the Arab conqueror Amr, to whom Alexandria fell in the year 640 of the Common Era, that of Octavian, that of Antony – or that of Alexander himself. And there was a hushed concentration among those assembled, as they checked and re-checked their gear – a concentration common to all who prepare to engage the unknown.

Now the wind again picked up. From the courtyard, one could look down into the long,

Although the campaign was scheduled for a calm period, bad weather occassionaly slowed the work. On one such stormy day, Stéphane Compoint chose to shoot the whole team, just above the site.

sloping, black, stone tunnel that led through an echoing darkness, around the base of the Fort — around the base of what had been the Pharos — to the water's edge. Through the iron bars of the distant first window of that tunnel, one could just make out, from the courtyard, the unmistakable and distinctly threatening roar of a rising sea. Waves slammed against the tunnel's outer wall, their recoil and repeat echoing through its vaulted barrel — these volleys of the sea's divisions. The consequent spume splattered through the window to the tunnel floor. Its facets recomposed there into a deranged approximation of the arched window through which they had passed. The glare of that slick pool on the stone floor was a much colder white than that of the sky, and it rendered the almost lightless tunnel a blacker black. The elements were not behaving as the team had optimistically hoped. Empereur said nothing, but would not have denied that — as toward the end of an Olympic competition from the highest diving platform — the degree of difficulty was mounting.

And time was running out. This was one of the last opportunities to produce the results for which Jean-Yves Empereur, Jean-Pierre Corteggiani, Georges Sarkassian and their team had been preparing for over a year, for which Asma el-Bakri had fought for over two years, for which Honor Frost and her dead friend had created the master demonstration more than a quarter century before.

Lou-Lou and Jeannot, the mechanics in charge of equipment, had exercised their skills and ensured all was primed for a testing undertaking. The photographer Stéphane Compoint prepared his ostensibly indestructible cameras with the most

A 3-D reconstruction of the Alexandria lighthouse, created by the production company Gédéon, and based on Herman Thiersch's plans. In this picture, the two colossal statues of Ptolemy and a Ptolemaic queen (bearing a resemblance to Isis Pharia) were added to the Thiersch plan. In reality, it seems the ramp and door were not on the east, but rather on the west side of the port.

delicate, precise attentions. The cinematographer Frédéric Labourasse mounted his diminutive video camera on his much larger film camera with repeated adjustments to the connection between them. All the while, he commented (very softly, as though the enemy were just beyond the back wall of the row of vaulted chambers, as though Rommel himself were surrounding the fort) at how often people remark on the fact that this high-tech equipment, which looks as though it might have been designed for the Voyager Spacecraft, meets his grip through the agency of a hardwood handle, carved to the specific contours of the human hand.

Le Corbusier wrote that something which is used by the hand tends to conform to the shape of the hand; that the larger an object becomes – the farther it departs, that is, from the scale of the hand – the closer it approaches a geometric form; that a city, finally, is pure geometry. Le Corbusier never saw the cameras of Frédérique Labourasse, but he had seen the stocks of rifles and the handles of pistols, and he had seen Alexandria – in Dinocrates' plan, in el-Falaky's reconstruction of that plan, and in actuality. He had stood at the intersection of the Sharia Horeyya and the Sharia Nebi Danyal, as Achilles Tatius had stood there in the Fifth Century of the Common Era, as Dinocrates himself had stood there eight centuries before him. He had known that the body of Alexander had lain precisely there in a translucent tomb for centuries, the pivot point of the known world.

The great architect of modernism knew, better than others of his time, how the cumulative achievement of the ages moves within us, how it

The colossal statue of Ptolemy prior to being pulled from the water.

Left: Jean-Pierre Corteggiani in front of the head of another colossal statue of Ptolemy.

Right: The colossal head, surrounded by slings, ready to be lifted to the surface.

leads us to comprehend within us a dignity greater than we ourselves, in a single lifetime, could attain, how that achievement, that dignity, and our knowledge of them are as integral to our identity as the conformation of our bones. He knew then also that there is no greater act than to retrieve, at whatever risk, the shards of that lost achievement, so that, through the recomposition of these shards, and the interpolation of the pieces we cannot retrieve, we know ourselves more fully, and for the first time.

The walls of the courtyard precluded the wind's entry, and the calm to be found there was undisturbed. The divers helped each other on with their wet suits and equipment. One after another, they looked up at the clear sky, gauging the direction and velocity of the few, small clouds. Then, two and three at a time — or, more often, singly — they turned and, with a confident ease, or the appearance of a confident ease, moved toward the tunnel's dark mouth.

The tunnel ended at a place where the foot of the rampart and the bedrock met, as Strabo had described it, at the edge of the open sea. The waves were now high, reaching up the

slope of bedrock to the rampart, and the huge slab of sloping rock, polished smooth over centuries, was dangerously slick. The rampart's wall of cut stone allowed no purchase, and the progress of the divers from rampart to sea was aided only by a rope which was itself already as slick as the rock and was proving distinctly precarious. Several divers slipped. One fell heavily and his head slammed against the rock slope. A gash opened on his forehead. The blood ran down his face and spilled onto his black wet suit. The red grew brighter against the black sheen and spread in a little delta down his chest. The shock of the accident brought home firmly to the others that real danger was present in this enterprise. Two other divers helped him to safety, but even an hour later, when the wound had been treated, he chose to sit by himself – stunned, a bit confused, disappointed that the day – and perhaps the entire campaign – was proceeding without him.

He would have taken no consolation from knowledge that the day was, in fact, proceeding only very slowly without him. He knew that the success of the mission depended on the cohesion of the team. His dedication was to that mission, to that team.

Left: The head rising from the water in front of the Fort Quayt Bey.

Right: Finally lying with the other pieces in a desalination basin which will be filled with water.

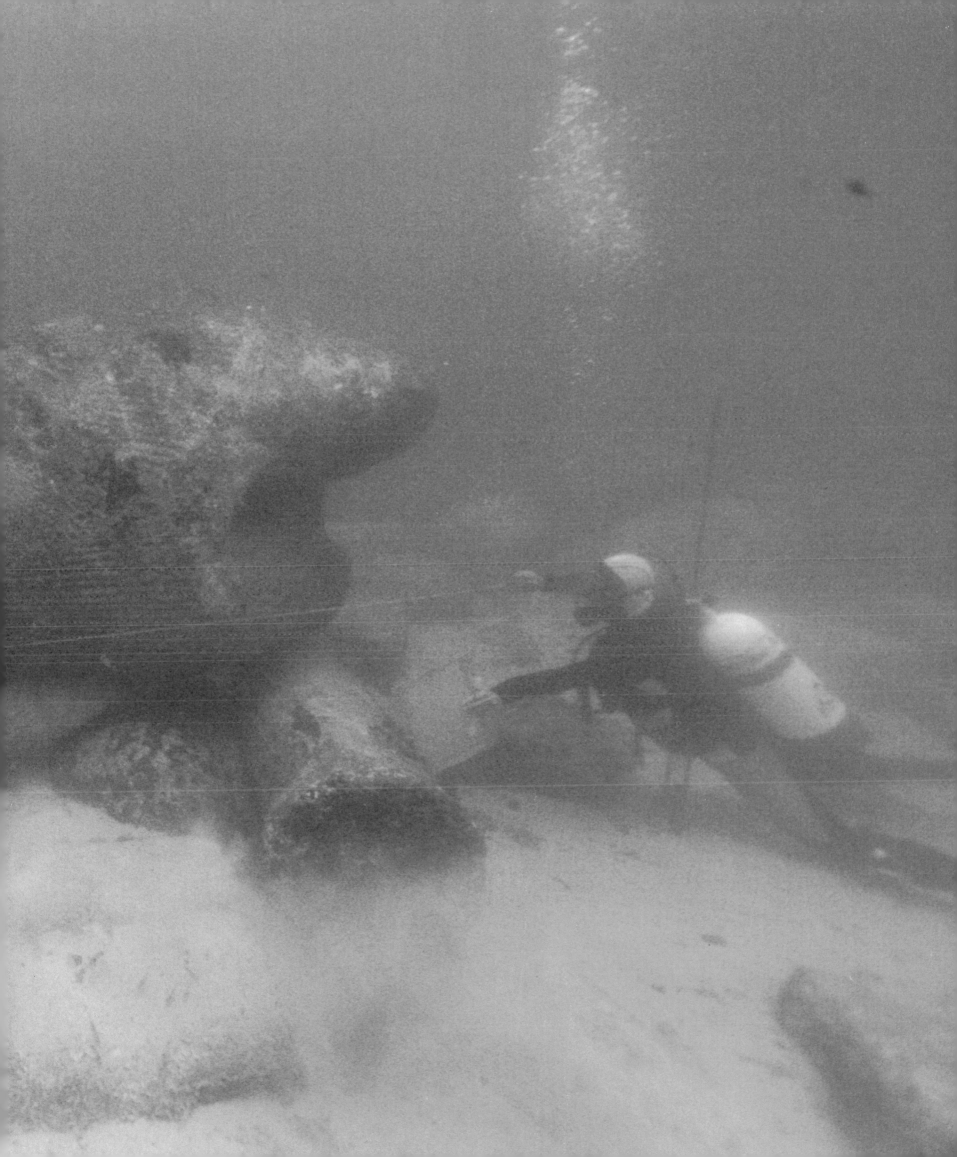

Pages 88-89: Sandrine Élaigne (left) and Dominique Allios measuring the statue of Ptolemy prior to drawing it for the Centre for Alexandrian Studies.

At the end of a dive the team members climb back up the ladder at the foot of the fort. On the left is Nathalie Gassiole, in the middle is Pierre Bruno, Snr, and on the right is Véronique François.

Tentatively, carefully, with the (marginal) help of the rope, each diver, after waiting for a wave's recoil, slid down the rock ledge and into the sea. He – or she, for several of them were women – then swam quickly away from the ledge, before the wave's return, or, if he had been too slow, submerged so he could swim under the wave, avoiding at least the full force of its collision with the rock. Once free of the breaking waves, in the trough or on the crest of a swell, each diver oriented himself to the others, to the shore and the distant barge. Empereur, again identifiable by his white cap and gloves, called, waved and pointed, as though directing a company of dancers. He was a precise choreographer, the Balanchine of Fort Quayt Bey. And yet he dealt with more variables than Balanchine – the changing, unpredictable winds, the heavy equipment, the weight and fragility of the pieces to be lifted, the sun's circuit, the surge and lethal gravity of the sea.

Honor Frost is drinking tea at the little café on the rampart. She looks out at the divers below, at the barge – still far off – and the rubber boat where the filmmakers bob and pitch. 'I think it will be a long wait. For Jean-Yves' sake, I hope it's a successful day. They're running out of time, you know. And money. Every day the barge is diverted costs them enormously. Even when it's supposed to show up for the team's use, it often doesn't. Walid says these things don't happen by accident in Egypt. I'm beginning to believe him.' Where there is bureaucracy, there is conspiracy, according to Walid el-Nasri, the Ibn Khaldun of the underwater set. And there are people whose only power is the power to deny you something. But the barge at least is visible today; it appears to be awaiting the call to move closer, to lower its winch once more to attach to a sleeping god.

'They tell me the first piece to be lifted today will be a headless sphinx.' Honor Frost takes a sip of her tea, savours it, continues. 'Ironic image. The sphinx has a lion's body for power and a man's head for intelligence. It is the protector of the dead. Of those in the Second Life. I'm not sure what good it can be without its head. Just another dumb beast. Can it still protect those in its charge? We shall see...on verra... '

On Encountering a Sleeping Colossus

The barge has begun to move closer. It is now perhaps a hundred metres away from the divers. Empereur or Corteggiani must have signalled to it. The divers have taken positions in a broad circle, treading water, occasionally calling to one another. In the centre of that circle, three divers descend two at a time, remain submerged for several minutes, before one rises to the surface with urgent words. Frost and the others on the rampart can hear his voice, but the crash of the waves, at this distance, drowns the sense of his words.

Clearly, as on October 4, the divers are about to harness something on the sea floor. The turbulence near the surface agitates the seabed, muddies the water, reduces visibility, increases still further the difficulty – the danger – of the work. The sea is rougher today than on the fourth, and, with the season changing, the weather deteriorating, the permit running out, the pressure on the team has reached its peak. Corteggiani descends, and then Empereur. When the latter rises to the surface, he signals to the winch barge, which moves closer still. It is now almost in position. Then a second, much smaller barge, also approaches. The intention, apparently, is to lift the piece with the larger, winch barge and then deposit it onto the deck of the smaller barge to be transported to the harbour. The larger barge therefore can remain in position for the next retrieval. But the two barges pitch violently at different angles, roll at different rhythms. Their two decks, in

The colossal statue and two divers amidst curious fish.

91

this rough sea, will never be perpendicular to the line of gravity at the same moment. How, under these conditions, will the winch on the deck of one barge deposit a large piece on the deck of the other without a dangerous – even lethal – mishap?

The winch barge is now in position. More divers circle closer. A balloon, like an enormous white jellyfish, marks the spot on the surface beneath which the object lies. One of the divers breaks the surface with a cable in his hand. The cable from the winch is lowered toward the diver. The other divers pull back as the heavy steel hook at the end of the winch cable swings like the ball at the end of a mace. The diver with the other

cable descends beneath the waves as the hook swings too close. Then he rises halfway out of the water and slams the hook at the end of his own cable onto that of the winch, leaps back, thrusts out his arms in a gesture of completion. Those on the rampart, at the instant of connection, hear a decisive 'clank', like the toll of a cracked bell: they are about to witness a momentous new hour in the history of Alexandria.

What emerges now from the sea (or begins to emerge) is large and linear, and of a reddish stone. If it is a sphinx, it is a huge one, and it is emerging upside down. But the shape which breaks the surface and then, with the swell of the sea and the pitch of the barge, descends out of sight, is more rounded than the base of a sphinx. It may be a massive column in the Egyptian style, or another architectural element – a carved lintel or parapet, worn by the rolling action of the currents and the waves. Whatever it is, it is as large as a killer whale, and as unwilling to forsake the still solace of the sea.

But eventually it does emerge, despite its recalcitrance and to the credit of the team, and rides like a powerful swimmer almost on top of the waves. It is the huge figure of a man, massive and muscular in form. It is a godly man, or indeed a god. The sheer authority of this figure, even half-seen as the winch chain pulls him from the sea and the sea pulls him back, unwilling to give him up, is overwhelming. Empereur had mentioned recently, in the library of the Centre for Alexandrian Studies, of how deeply he is moved by encountering a great stone figure beneath the sea. The profound thrill of it. Now there is no doubt in the minds of those who heard him say these words, who observe from the rampart and the café of the Fort, that it was of this unquestionably magnificent colossus that he had spoken with such unashamed admiration.

Later, on the quay, Jean-Pierre Corteggiani would run his hand over the sophisticated modelling of the sculpture's musculature, and he would marvel at the sheer skilled artistry of it, at the power and the utter confidence of conception and execution, and he would wonder out loud as to who, in Ptolemaic times, occupied that place in the collective imagination where the regal and the godly coincide: might this be a figure of the deified Ptolemy I Soter, commissioned by his son? Might it be one of a pair with a sculpture of Berenice, his queen, not yet recovered – or recovered and incorrectly identified? It was too soon to tell, but these were among the many possibilities that moved through his mind, as those who were so much less well-informed merely marveled at this gift that had entered their lives – those who, like Jean-Pierre Corteggiani, were moved to the core of their being.

One of the monumental blocks being towed to the inner part of the port. The inflated balloons remain attached until the tow boat reaches land.

'Our Jean-Yves certainly does have a sense of theatre, doesn't he.' This is not a question. Honor Frost permits, for the moment, no demurral from her admiration, which has become suddenly proprietorial.

And now the colossus, in a mythic stasis, hangs above his city and the sea. '... Thou foster child of silence and slow time,' Keats wrote in his *Ode on a Grecian Urn*, as if with this instant in mind.

After the initial flurry of excited chatter, a quiet pervades those on the rampart. All are motionless, staring at the image before them, at the huge figure suspended above the waves, above Alexandria itself. What they see before them is (they are beginning to comprehend) something of a unique and almost impossible majesty, something they alone of all those living on the earth, of all the city's inhabitants since the time of Alexander, have been chosen to behold. A humility, bit by bit, now pervades them also: why is it they who have been chosen? And what is the responsibility of their witness? A few of them may know that 'grace' somewhere is defined as an undeserved gift from God. All would now no doubt comprehend Beckett's statement in Molloy: 'To restore silence is the role of objects'.

The majestic statue rises symbolically above Alexandria.

A decision has been taken: the second barge is waved off; no attempt will be made to land so large a figure on that wildly pitching deck. Instead, the winch barge will take it, suspended from its cable, into the Eastern Harbour. The winch barge turns slowly, and its stately progress, regal and deliberate, seems timed to the irreducible gravity of its mission: after a more than millennial repose beneath the sea, a colossus, riding just above the waves, glides to his haven across the harbour from the submerged palace of Cleopatra, the last Ptolemy of his probable line; a god king prepares to reclaim his terrestrial realm.

Right: Alessandro Sturla, assistant to Stéphane Compoint, playing hide and seek with the colossal female bust.

The Taming of The Sphinx

The day proceeds. Honor Frost – from the rampart, from the café, from the quay, from the pavilion in the courtyard, from the vaulted chamber where her own diving gear awaits her next descent (when, as the day before, she again will join Empereur and Corteggiani in the realm she charted when they were children in France) – observes the action and sees within it the actions of all who have sought knowledge beneath the surface of this sea, since before the Second War. They have sought that knowledge in Egypt and Palestine, Israel and Lebanon, Syria and Turkey, Cyprus and Greece, Albania, Montenegro, Croatia, Italy and Sicily, France and Spain, the countries of the Maghreb, and, finally, Libya – which shares a desert with Egypt. That desert has swallowed whole armies without a trace, and it has witnessed, in one of its oases, the anointing of a twenty-three year-old Macedonian Son of the King of the Gods.

'Mare Nostrum', the Romans called it. 'Our Sea' indeed, but few among them knew it as Honor Frost knows it, each jut of rock and tenacious patch of wind-bent scrub along the

One of the twelve sphinxes prior to being lifted in the October 1995 campaign.

shore, each fjord, grotto and calanque, the perpetual forming of clouds over the somber cone of Stromboli, the granular black wastes where the Lipari meet the sea, the endless sands beneath which the Greek cities of North Africa still repose, the submerged sandbars themselves that have claimed so many ships, the starved hills' brown spines from which Frost so often has looked down. She has looked down and seen so many towns diced white by the sea verge, as the gods diced Rachotis once before the eyes of a Macedonian boy-man who read in those jumbled cubes the germ of a city that would encompass all of which the human race was capable.

The human race this day has proved itself capable of retrieving the fallen mantle of Kemal Abu el-Saadat. It is this evidence – this mounting evidence – that Honor Frost has sought, even as she has offered, in her rambling, often wry accounts of dives in Lebanon and Cyprus and Sicily, the framework of anecdotal history and science in which the current dives one day will take their place. And she has not been disappointed. She returns to the café on the rampart. She adjusts the brim of her straw peasant's hat, which she bought in China, to protect her English skin from the Egyptian sun. A waiter who, after more than a week now, has developed a proprietorial, even avuncular concern for this lady three times his age, adjusts the large umbrella at the next table in a tender gesture of protective intention. It is not hard to see how one of his ancestors might have done the same for the equally intelligent Cleopatra, as she observed the Battle of Actium.

The only sphinx to have retained his head, with Jean-Yves Empereur on the right, Samah Ramsès in the middle and Pierre Bruno on the left.

The arrival on land of a sphinx dating from the reign of Ramses II.

The Alexandrian forces at the Battle of Fort Quayt Bey, in 1995 of the Common Era, are, happily, much better organised, their strategy more thoughtfully considered, their 'Antony' more temperate, more deliberate – more resourceful, even, in improvisation – than they were in 31 BCE. Today there is no Anubis barking over the Alexandrian fleet of two barges and a rubber dinghy. Only a small cat purring as it rubs itself, from time to time, against Honor Frost's leg.

The wind picks up again and joins forces with the sea to create a fearsome foe for the divers. The swells culminate, sporadically, in waves now breaking far from shore, and these waves arc back in a spindrift foam that the wind then carries forward, parallel to the earth's curve, until, in an atomised meteor shower of water and of salt, it impedes the vision of the divers through their face masks once they break the surface.

'Each piece they bring up stirs up the mud below, creates a soup for those who must come after', Honor Frost explains. 'Each successive piece is therefore harder to bring up. And now this wind. Makes it hard to see even at the surface. It was already hard to hear.' She adjusts the brim of her Chinese hat, this time to deflect the wind. 'Appalling conditions. A Turkish coffee is in order. My fuel, you know.' She turns her head to hail the waiter, but he is already there beside her, bowing in ascent.

The three ton sphinx is wrenched from the seabed, then placed in a desalination tub.

The cat jumps onto her lap. The waiter tries to shew it away. 'No. Let her stay, let her stay. This is a great day for felines, after all.'

And indeed, two sphinxes, albeit headless, are recovered as the day progresses, along with a huge lintel or parapet which must be from a building of monumental scale – the Pharos?. A papyriform column capital also has been recovered – which confirms, to Corteggiani and Empereur, decades of conjecture regarding the presence, at Alexandria, of Egyptian along with Greek stylistic modes in the architecture of the Ptolemies.

The sun continues its descent, and with each extension of the shadow of the Fort across the water, the light that falls upon the faces of the mariners on the barges, the photographers and cameramen in the rubber boat, the archaeologists in the sea and on the barges and the rampart and the sea wall becomes a deeper and more luminous gold. It is as though they themselves are the source of this rich light, and the exaggerated length of the shadows of their bodies accentuates the magnitude of their every gesture.

Another post from the doorway of the lighthouse before it lands at the foot of Fort Quayt Bey.

It accentuates also the tension within the team, for time is running out, and there still is another piece to raise today. The wind on the sea does not abate. The two barges pitch again in wild disjuncture. The violent speed with which they tilt one way and then the next defies prediction, unleashes the lethal potential of all that is not bolted down. A balloon appears on the water. The large circle of divers is wary and alert: the second barge also comes in close now; something else for the divers to look out for. The heads of the divers turn swiftly to keep the barges and one another in just relation. Their gestures seem much quicker than earlier in the day. There is a

Their proportions allow the pieces to be dated. Walid Nazmi is measuring the only sphinx with an intact head.

vigilant defiance about the divers now – a defiance of the sea's rough action in the wind, of the lethal pitching of the barges, of the crazed swinging of the winch chain, of the dying of the light.

Suddenly, a connection. Soon something will rise. Two divers surface near the rising cable. On the deck of the smaller barge, Walid el-Nasri and Asma el-Bakri await, with the seamen, the object's emergence. And it does emerge, with a wild burst, like a missile from a submarine, through the waves. Then, as though come to life , it writhes and twists in what seems a murderous rage. It is a sphinx, a large one, but no dumb beast: its head is intact, and the 'twenty centuries of stony sleep' from which it just has wakened have wrenched it also from its sacred charge. The sphinx is guardian of those in the Second Life, of the sea floor's denizens whom Empereur's team disturbs. He will not go gently out of that good night, into exile from his trust. Like the great hook at the end of the winch chain, but magnified five thousand times, he himself becomes a huge and swinging weapon. The chain could snap and he could fall, crushing seamen or divers as he tumbles back below. His several tons could lurch back at the winch barge, bend or even snap the steel members of the winch itself. Perhaps it was unwise to raise him in this sea.

Perhaps. But here he is. The sea now is too wild to dangle him like the colossus all the way to port. And this time it seems less dangerous also to keep him from the winch barge he might damage. The decision is made to deposit him, as gingerly as possible (if at all possible) onto the smaller barge where a crew awaits with boards and cables to secure him. And not just any crew. Seasoned mariners to be sure, but also Asma el-Bakri, she who may have been the first to encounter this sphinx beneath the sea. ('We have had many conversations down below, he and I. We are old friends. Confidants.') Walid el-Nasri is also on the barge – the

marine chemist, advocate of Coastal Zone Management, Navy diver, Kung Fu practitioner, national team member in water polo and (field) hockey – he who, in one of Stéphane Compoint's most mysterious photos, which has been published around the world, summing up the spirit of the campaign, appears to be interviewing this very sphinx at the bottom of the sea, pen and clipboard in hand. ('What on earth is Walid doing in this photo?,' someone asks Jean-Pierre Corteggiani. 'Posing', comes the response.)

The arrival of their 'old friend' is hardly reassuring. The disjointed pitching of the decks of the two barges is now even more violent making the team's aim increasingly far from realisation.. The unknown toward which the divers were heading, as the day began, when they entered the long tunnel's dark mouth, has come to this complete uncertainty. The winch operator tries manfully to lower the sphinx onto the smaller barge's deck. The wild pitch of the two decks makes the sphinx hit once and bounce at an angle through the air. Several tons of carved stone fly toward Walid, who leaps back – agile as a Kung Fu master and bent on self-preservation – just far enough. 'The first one to know the measure of far and near wins,' Sun Tzu wrote, in *The Art of War*. Walid knows this, and Newton's Laws of Motion.

The sphinx returns through the air and like a fighter landing too fast on a carrier, slams the deck as Walid approaches, this time flying off at a different angle. Walid again jumps back, but this time – if for only half a second – he has laid his hand, gently, on the wet, stone back. Sun Tzu again: 'Using order to deal with the disorderly, using calm to deal with the clamorous, is mastering the heart.' But is there, in Egyptian (or even Chinese) myth, a precedent for what Walid would calm, for the airborne sphinx? Or is Empereur's team creating a new species?

Head to head between the sphinx and Walid Nazmi, in the photograph by Stéphane Compoint which was seen all around the world.

Several more attempts fail. The number of angles at which the sphinx can avoid a landing that will insure his capture appears infinite; the number of ways in which he can swing his bulk to successfully crush his 'old friends' seems equally without limit. He appears to alight for a second, and Asma el-Bakri leaps on his back. The winch barge lurches, she leaps off, and the sphinx is again in the air. He twists, and his huge stone head almost grazes hers. A few more inches and it would have crushed her skull. He alights again, and Walid attempts to subdue him while four seamen approach with ropes and with boards on top of which they would secure their stone prize. The two decks again lurch at different angles, different rates. The sphinx swings left and would crush Walid if he did not leap backward. This time, however,

Pages 104-105: The calcite block, an offering to the gods, from the reign of Sethi II, imprisoned in the nets as it is drawn from the water.

the sphinx is on the deck. The seamen move in to restrain it while it is calm. Asma and Walid each grab a rope. At last they have their wild man-beast where they want him. He is again pinned in his eternal crouch. Asma jumps on the creature's back again. She grabs his huge stone head and places her own against it. She appears to be whispering into the stone ear. What may the Conscience of Egypt be saying to the ancient stone Protector of the Second Life?

More boards and ropes come forward. The sphinx, at last, is the captive of Alexandrians – who have known, since Eratosthenes, the measure of far and near. Later, on the quay, the long-tranquil, finally violent life of the sphinx, torn from his duty to the dead, will seem to have ebbed from him. His stone skin will be bruised – scraped but somehow, as if by a miracle, not chipped in this valiant battle, fought after centuries on the peaceful sea bed . His remains be a dignified if detached composure, like that of a great chief of the Sioux under guard in a Cavalry fort. His commitment to the battle, to the protection of those in his charge, has been absolute. Now he shall detach himself from the result that he cannot control. He shall await his destiny with a patrician indifference.

Honor Frost has said nothing during the battle for the sphinx. Now that it is over, she rises wearily from her chair. Tomorrow she shall dive again, as so many times before. As she rises, the cat leaps from her lap, takes a few steps, and looks back up at her. 'Ahhh, my little sphinx', Honor Frost says, looking down, and one hears in her voice the full, sad, compassionate wisdom of a lifetime of engagement with the unknown and all its risks. 'And what do you think of your noble ancestor now?'

Submission

The wooden object was shaped like a mihrab – a prayer niche – and one of the seamen laid it on the winch barge's deck, as he might a prayer rug on which a representation of the niche (that rectangle of space surmounted by a pointed arch) is the principal figure. He laid it on the barge's deck, pointing it in the direction of Mecca.

Like all mariners, he had assimilated the systems of Euclid, of Aristarchus, of Eratosthenes: the science of Alexandria was subconsciously intuitive within him. Like all Muslims, he was an infallible navigator of the direction of true worship.

This was not, however, a rug. Rather, it was a structure perhaps a metre and a half in length, nailed together out of several boards. At one end, what would have been the curved arch was a wooden triangle. The whole thing curiously had somewhat the aspect of a child's sled. The bracing at right angles below the upper layer of narrow boards kept its upper surface a couple inches above the deck, so that he could kneel on it even when the deck was awash with salt water and still keep dry. The direction of Mecca was to the east and a little to the south, so that the sun, barely above the horizon at that hour, was behind him.

With the battle for the sphinx at an end, with the winch barge about to turn to the east, to the harbour entrance, the day's last flood of October sunlight bathed (with deepest gold and a luminous reflectance) the weathered wood and rusted metal of the shed beside which, in the narrow space between it and the gunwale, the mariner stood, and sat, and knelt, and prostrated himself in the attitudes of Muslim prayer. The wall beside him was as vibrant as the background of an icon of the Copts, as burnished as a sacred treasure of the Jews.

Head of a sphinx dating from Psamtik II. The body of this sphinx, covered with hieroglyphics, was also lifted during the autumn 1995 campaign.

The very action of the mariner's prayer slowed the action of the day, until the two were one to those watching from the rampart – were one with the rhythm – the stately, undulant rhythm – of the swelling of the sea. Those on the rampart could not hear, above the waves, the words of his prayer, but their gravity, and the dignity of submission, were in his every motion. The dignity of submission. To the one god in whom all yearning of the spirit is resumed. A form of that submission is the soul risk by which artists became agencies through whom the colossus of the god-king took visible–tangible–form; and the hybrid god Serapis; and the goddess Isis; and the guardian Sphinx; and even the great Amun, whom the Greeks call Zeus.

All those gods of the Egyptians, his forebears, were mere approximations to the archetype, our mariner (in different, direct, and reverent words) would have us know. The words those on the rampart could not hear were words 'in the language of recitation', as the poet Adonis26 calls his native Arabic, and what is recited is revelation – the revelation to Muhammed that, among so much else, there is but this one God, He who is the Compassionate, the Merciful, the loving God of the Christians and their prophet Jesus, the just God of the Jews and their father Abraham. Indeed, it was to a house which Abraham had built, with his son Ishmael, on the site of a shrine which Adam had constructed, toward which the man on the barge, floating above the strewn remnants of Pharos, was directing his prayer: to the Ka'aba in Mecca. Pharos, Pharaoh – even this word for 'Great House' came, the lexicographers tell us, ultimately, from the language of Abraham.

The action of the man on the winch barge, so much the opposite of the prideful image Shakespeare gives us of the last Ptolemaic queen – 'The barge she sat on, like a burnished throne'27 – brings home the transformation the great Cavafy had effected, when the god of the queen's consort Antony becomes the city itself, becomes Alexandria. For Cavafy, too, brings us a single god, who has suffused the city and all within it – a god whose kingdom is within each being. (And this is but one of the concepts we find so difficult to accept. The Prophet Muhammed said, 'We have more right to doubt than Abraham did when he said, "Lord, show me how you quicken the dead." God said, "Do you not believe?" Abraham replied, "Oh, yes! But it would reassure my heart."' 28).

The work of the sculptors who produced the colossus, the sphinx, the noble torso, was an attempt to register the eternal, the sacred that is within each of us. ('Namaste', the Hindus say in greeting, 'The sacred which is within me honours the sacred which is within you'.) The sculptors too, without knowing it, were preparing the way for the humble mariner on the winch barge, for the revelation that is the one God – the Compassionate, the Merciful – who moves through the artist in his making. Somebody once asked Matisse if he believed in God. 'Yes,' the painter answered, 'when I'm working'.

On a Rooftop at the Edge of Shalalat

In the cool November air, from the rooftop of the building which houses the Centre for Alexandrian Studies, Jean-Yves Empereur watches the last light fade from the western sky. A football game continues in the stadium across the street, and the floodlights – 'phares

On land, the topographers Xavier Ablain (left) and Patrick Deleuze direct the divers who are measuring.

109

à iodes' – have just come on above their tapering steel towers. He considers these towers, the blaze atop them, he considers how far back, in the history of Alexandria, this phenomenon recedes. Skeletal structures now, steel members diagonally braced, no skin of stone about them. But the principle is the same: go high with the light to illumine, with equanimity, the distant contest – be it with the team of a rival city or the rage of a recalcitrant sea.

Indeed, the crowd's sporadic roar exaggerates a decent pass to the status of a goal, for the opponent today is Cairo, and each advance, however tentative, has the taste of revenge about it. The Ancient Capital versus the Modern Capital, the repository of ageless values versus the arena of mindless growth. Between the crowd's excesses, the huge tonal range and rhythmic complexity of the interplay of Egyptian automobile horns reminds the inhabitant of this eyrie that, below, the world continues. From another direction, the muffled sound of music, vibrant and self-confident, rises through the trees from the few open windows of a restaurant where a wedding reception is underway. Celebration surrounds the high solitude of the man on the roof. 'The sounds drift in.' Wallace Stevens wrote. 'The buildings are remembered./ The life of the city never lets go, nor do you/ Ever want it to.' Nor do you ever want it to.

Celebration in fact does seem the order of the day. The pioneering explorations of Kemal Abu el-Saadat and Honor Frost come back to him, and even the death of Saadat in the wreck of Napoleon's flagship, in the sea off Aboukir, seems in a way redeemed; the repeated alarms sounded by Asma el-Bakri come back to him, and the image of 'the Cultural Conscience of Egypt' whispering like Hector, Tamer of Horses, into the stone ear of a captive sphinx; he recalls the always sage articulations of scholarly – and ethical – concern from Mustafa el-Abbadi, whose nuanced mind dissects a problem with the precision of a surgeon; he brings to mind the accuracy, the grace, the heroic, calm persistence of the writings of Hala Halim; he smiles in satisfaction at the relentless cartographic ingenuity of Xavier Ablain and Christophe Regni; he marvels at the acts of luminous witness from the photographer Stéphane Compoint and the filmmaker Andrew Snell the contributions of these and of more than a score of

Left: The divers accompany an enormous block lifted to the surface by balloons.

View of the port and corniche from the French consulate in Alexandria.

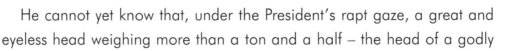

Pages 112-113: Fragment of an
obelisk dating from the reign of
pharoah Apriés (6th century BC).

others have brought a moment's victory of sorts. More than a decent pass, more even than a single goal, but the battle indeed continues.

The great spirit and electric insights of Jean-Pierre Corteggiani, the always evocative – sometimes provocative – reflections of Georges Sarkassian may retire from the field only briefly. 'There is no flight after victory,' Muhammed said, 'but struggle and planning.' There is the struggle and challenge to wrest, through study and analysis, solid knowledge from the pieces already rescued. There is the planning of the next campaigns.

Empereur cannot yet know that, with the commencement of the Spring Campaign, in April, 1996, the President of France will stand upon the quay, that he will resume the lapsed imperative of his predecessor Napoleon, the cultural imperative that has remained, in death as in life, the object of Kemal Abu el-Saadat's now wordless exhortation.

Empereur cannot yet know that Jacques Chirac will come to Fort Quayt Bey in homage to the achievement of Alexandria, of Egypt, of Hellenism, of the courageous enterprise of those who dive to save the stones that are so significant a portion of the world's memory.

He cannot yet know that, while the President looks on, still another sphinx of Pharaonic provenance will break the surface headless to be subdued upon the barge.

He cannot yet know that, under the President's rapt gaze, a great and eyeless head weighing more than a ton and a half – the head of a godly king – will rise also on the chain of the barge's winch. He cannot know that the water will stream from the huge granite skull as it turns in the breeze until its dark sockets engage the mortal gaze of its fellow chief of state. Will this not be, most probably, the head of the first Ptolemy, who commissioned the Pharos completed in his son's reign? Will this not be the head which once sat upon the neck of the colossus retrieved the previous October? How long has the rolling action of the sea ground this head's once proud features against the sand?

'... *Et la mer à la ronde roule son bruit de crânes sur les grèves...* ', wrote St.-John Perse. '... *And the rounding sea rolls its sound of skulls on the shores...* '

Empereur, finally, cannot yet know that the great head soon will rest upon the shore, that the President will touch the shadows that were its eyes. Why is it that we impute a special

wisdom to the blind, a parallel and much deeper vision to those who, like Tiresias, cannot see? Perhaps it is because they are less susceptible to distraction by fugitive phenomena. Whatever the reason, one can but hope that this Ptolemy's mute head – for its mouth also has been ground away by the sand – will impart some particle of accumulated wisdom to Chirac, across the two thousand three hundred years that it will have taken for the trajectory of a President of France and that of an ancient King of Egypt to intersect – in accordance with every law of Eratosthenes and Euclid – at Alexandria, at the northern edge of Egypt.

And still, one suspects, Jean-Yves Empereur cannot help but feel, in the cool November evening, a satisfaction verging on celebration rise within him. Thirty-four pieces have been removed from the sea in the Campaign of 1995. Gods, goddesses, kings, queens, the very sphinxes have risen through the waves. The colossal body of a godly king, in powerful repose,

The transport of an 11.4 ton colossus through the streets of Alexandria to the desalination tanks.

Part of the team of divers standing in front of fragments of the lighthouse. From front to back: Jean-Yves Empereur, Jean-Pierre Corteggiani, Xavier Ablain, Pierre Bruno, Benoît Poinard, Nathalie Gassiole, Walid Nazmi, Jean Curnier, Annick Chele, Robert Leffy, Christophe Requi, Tarek Abou el-Ela, Mohamed el-Sayed, Mohamed Mustafa, Alain Peton, Dominique Allios.

has been seen moving on a flatbed truck among the Fiats and Skodas of the commercial centre of a city that was once his own, so long before it took its current form. The people pause and turn as their history passes before them. The majestic torso of October Fourth moves by, and a woman in a head scarf steps to the entry of her jewelry shop, observes, in silence, the somber grandeur of those heroic breasts in their passage through the street's monoxide gloom. A sphinx approaches, poised in vigilance to its charge as protector of these denizens of the Second Life, who precede it through the city – and a child is raised to its father's shoulders, to be told later, perhaps, what it has seen.

Through these figures' return, through this incomparable procession, the God re-enters the city. To Cavafy, the God who abandoned Antony was Alexandria itself, the city whose own divinity derives from the Son of Amun, this Alexander whose very mission, the Muslims tell us, was divine. And the divinity of that mission, we must conclude, was derived from the One God, the Compassionate, the Merciful.

The music has entered the street from the restaurant beyond the trees, next door to the building which houses, on its seventh floor, the Centre for Alexandrian Studies. The bride and groom, it seems, are about to leave. The ecstatic trilling of the women rises to the rooftop, undiminished in its vibrancy, and Cavafy's words are remembered:

'… when suddenly you hear
an invisible procession going by
with exquisite music, voices… '

As the great stone figures re-enter the city, the God effectively re-enters the city, and Alexandria again is one with the glory – the shining example – of its past. Their long night journey through water has come to an end. The symbolism of the journey taken by the artefacts which once adorned the seventh wonder of the ancient world should not be lost on the people of Egypt. It was by water that the Pharaohs themselves passed into the next life. The complex process of ritual embalmment ensured the body of the dead king or queen remained intact beyond this life and into the next. For the stone figures of the Pharos lighthouse, it was the sea itself which acted as their protector on the journey. The spirit of these figures again marries those kindred stones the ages have composed into the city's weary buildings. That spirit suffuses the elegant façades that line the Corniche; it pervades the souks and fetid alleys, the crumbling stucco of aging cinemas, the massed domes of the great mosques and the Cathedral of the Copts; it moves upward until it enters the Serapeion's high remnants; it descends into the catacombs of el-Shogafa; it invades the poignant motley of the

one still-standing wall of an apartment building that has been torn down – only to reveal yet another unforeseen – unforeseeably significant – ruin; it enters, finally, the ancient, welcoming stones of the theatre of Kom el-Dik. It is near here that the figures, salvaged by Jean-Yves Empereur and his committed team from almost certain destruction beneath the breakwater, undergo the baths of desalination that are their final purifying rite – washing them clean of many hundreds of years of sea salt.

Their long night sea journey has ended, to be sure, but when will their terrestrial mission also be complete? Already they have returned the world's attention to the achievement that is Alexandria. Already they have precipitated the Government's decision to remove the breakwater that obstructed further inquiry into their realm beneath the sea. Already their emergence has caused the entire coast from Alexandria to Alamein – replete as it is with civilizations latent beneath the sands – to be reclassified as an archeological zone. The expedition has achieved all that it could ever have reasonably wished for, but there is always more

When will the sewers finally be diverted from the city's coast and their effluent purified? When may we expect that the vision of Professor Hassan el-Banna—a vision espoused also by Honor Frost, el-Abbadi, Halim, el-Bakri, Jean-Pierre Corteggiani, Georges Sarkassian, and Jean-Yves Empereur himself – become a reality: When will the undersea archaeological preserve they envisage finally be created? When, in sum, may these great stone figures return to the strewn remnants of Pharos, to the care of a clarified sea?

The head lifted in April 1996 is placed with the colossal statue in a desalination tank. It will stay there for six to nine months, soaking in water that is changed every week.

Following pages: President Jacques Chirac with the head of the colossal statue lifted from the sea in April 1996. The head belongs to the 11.4 ton statue found in October of 1995.

CHRONOLOGY OF EXPLORATION
OF THE PHAROS SITE

1961

Kemal Abu el-Saadat, accomplished diver and amateur archaeologist, discovers sculptures from the Ptolemaic period in the waters off Fort Quayt Bey. Rebutted by the archaeological establishment, he convinces the Egyptian Navy to assist by removing a colossal female figure from the sea bed. The so-called Isis Pharia (from *Pharos*) now resides in the Garden of Alexandria's Maritime Museum.

1968

Saadat convinces UNESCO to assist by mapping the locations of the most important of the many pieces he has discovered in the waters near the Fort, which stands on the site of Pharos, the ancient lighthouse of Alexandria. UNESCO sends the geologist Vladimis Nesteroff and the archaeologist and diver Honor Frost to Alexandria. She and Saadat, triangulating with lengths of string, locate several pieces which Frost later delineates in the first plan of the ruins on this site.

1976

Frost publishes her sketches of figures she saw beneath the sea and a description of the site in the journal, *Nautical Archaeology*.

1993

Asma el-Bakri, an Egyptian filmmaker, dives at the site in preparation of a film about the Greco-Roman Museum of Alexandria; she is alarmed to find that huge blocks of concrete have been dropped by the Government on the submerged sculptures and architectural pieces in order to create a breakwater. She enlists the support of the architect Muhammed Awad and others in mounting a protest against the construction and in alerting the world to the importance of the site.

1994

An Egyptian French team is organized under the Classical Archaeologist, Dr Jean-Yves Empereur, and his Centre for Alexandrian Studies, in conjunction with Dr Nicolas Grimal, head of the French Institute for Oriental Archaeology in Cairo. The French film production company Gédéon, under Stéphane Millière, provides impetus to the effort to further explore the site and rescue the more significant pieces. Gédéon provides financial support and also enlists that of the Fondation Elf, the Fondation Electricité de France, Leica, and other funders. An effort begins, under Empereur's leadership, to further explore and map the underwater site.

1995

A Spring campaign is undertaken by Empereur, his colleagues, the Egyptologists Jean-Pierre Corteggiani and Georges Sarkassian, and a team of more than twenty archaeologists, cartographers, oceanographers and divers. The purpose is to further explore and map the site, using the most advanced methods, including sonar and satellites, and to begin preparation of the most significant pieces for removal from the sea bed. Gédéon commissions the filmmaker Andrew Snell to create a documentary on the project for presentation on television around the world. The campaign continues through May and June until it is suspended for the summer to permit analysis of findings.

1995

An Autumn Campaign begins spectacularly with the removal of a magnificent female torso on October Fourth. The event is covered by much of the world's press and the project catches the imagination of the public in not only Egypt and France, but much of Europe, America and Japan. Thirty-four significant pieces are removed, with Honor Frost joining Empereur's team for the effort. Their analysis may lead to significant revisions in scholarly understanding of Ptolemaic Alexandria and its artistic achievement.

1996

The Egyptian Government orders the dismantling of the breakwater and its reconstruction away from the ruins of the Pharos complex. They also designate the coast from Alexandria to the Libyan Border an Archaeological Zone. Empereur presents his findings in a lecture at the Institute de France. A second Spring Campaign is undertaken. Jacques Chirac, President of France, visits the site on April Eight, as the great head of a Ptolemaic king, most likely Ptolemy I Soter, is withdrawn from the sea. Gédéon's film, entitled *The Seventh Wonder of the World*, in reference to the lighthouse, is presented on French television to general acclaim. Empreur and his team continue their campaign through the month of June, while planning the campaigns to come.

HISTORICAL CHRONOLOGY

HISTORY

Before Jesus Christ

3500 to 3001
3100 approx. The Scorpion-King is the only known Pharoah of the pre-dynastic period
3000 to 2501 King Menes unites Upper und Lower Egypt and, according to Heroditus, founds Memphis

3000 to 2501
2690 approx. Old kingdom
2613 to 2589 approx. Invasion of Palestine by the Egyptians

2500 to 2001
Isis and Osiris cult established
2050 Beginning of the Middle Kingdom
2006 approx. First expeditions to Libya and Nubia

2000 to 1501
1720 approx. Invasion of Egypt by the Hyksos
Egypt control Crete and the Aegean seas
1580 approx. Amosis I liberates Egypt from Hyksos, founds New Kingdom

1500 to 1001
1472 approx. Thutmose III extends empire to banks of Euphrates and Upper Nile
1370 approx. Akhnaton and Nefertiti move capital from Thebes to Amarna. Found the cult of Aton
1361 approx. Tutankhamen reinstates multiple gods, moves the capital to Memphis
1324 approx. Ramses II is Pharaoh. Signs peace with the Hittites
1250 approx. Hebrew Exodus

EGYPTIAN SOCIETY

Before Jesus Christ

3500 to 3001
Oldest known use of numbers
First use of geometry for land survey
First evidence of bread making
First limited use of native metals (gold, copper)
Appearance of weaving (linen) and basketry
Traces of sedentary agriculture and animal rearing

3000 to 2501
First traces of the domestication of beef, pigs, sheep, geese and dogs
2800 approx. First bi-level balances
Farming of cereals (wheat, millet, barley) and of vegetables (lentils, beans, onions, chick peas)
Appearance of hoe and the swing-plough

2500 to 2001
2500 approx. Invention of a motion system for welling water
2160 First vertical looms
Frequent use of bronze
Expanding use of papyrus
Development of mummification under the Ive dynasty

2000 to 1501
2000 approx. First studies of gynaecology and veterinary science found on papyrus
Writing system founded on a twenty-four letter alphabet
1700,1600 First fabrication of glass coloured with mineral oxides
First use of the wheel

1500 to 1001
1500 Appearance of the enamelled brick
1425 Development of beekeeping
Use of obelisks as sun-dials
First rules concerning beer
1300 approx. first horses in Egypt

AROUND EGYPT

Before Jesus Christ

3500 to 2001
3500 First appearance of writing in Mesopotamia
2750 Founding of Tyre by the Phoenicians
2700 Beginnings of Cretan civilization
2100 Europe: start of Bronze Age

2000 to 1501
1900 Founding of Babylon (Mesopotamia)
1900 Founding of Jerusalem
1800 Europe: Bronze Age

1500 to 1001
1450 approx. Founding of New Hittite Empire
1400 Expansion of Mycenian civilization in the Mediterranean. First Greek writing
1300 Hebrews arrive in Palestine.
1050 Spreading of Greek population throughout the Mediterranean. The Aegean sea has become a 'Greek lake'

HISTORY	EGYPTIAN SOCIETY	AROUND EGYPT
1000 to 501 927 approx. Jerusalem conquered and pillaged by the Pharaoh Sheshonk I 675 approx. Invasion of Egypt by the Assyrians; destruction of Memphis (671 approx.) and of Thebes 525 Cambyses II, King of Persia, having conquered Egypt, crowns himself King of Egypt	**1000 to 501** 712 Iron metallurgy Traces of poppy cultivation Wigs used by Egyptian aristocracy (1st dynasty), and in Assyria	**1000 to 501** 1000 to 850 arrival of Etruscans in Italy 960 Solomon king of Israel. Construction of the Jerusalem Temple 900 Arrival of the Celts in Gaul 814 Founding of Carthage 753 Founding of Rome 750 Europe: Iron Age 650 Founding of Byzantium by the Greeks 604 Nabushodonosor II, king of Babylon, leads the Neobabylonian empire to its greatest height 600 Founding of Massilia (Marseille) by Phocaean Greeks 600 Italy: high point of Etruscan power 587 Destruction of the Jerusalem Temple by Nabushodonosor II 510 Founding of the Roman Empire 508 Establishment of democracy in Athens
500 to 332 356 Birth of Alexander the Great, son of Philip II of Macedonia 340 His father absent, Alexander the Great governs 336 Assasination of Philip II 334 Alexander crosses the Hellespont and wins against the Persians in the Battle of Granique 332 Alexander defeats Persia at Issus and Guagamela; conquers Tyre and Jerusalem. He enters Egypt and founds Alexandria. Greeks will rule Egypt for the following 250 years	**500 to 332** 332 approx. Statue of egyptian Serapis by Bryaxis	**500 to 332** 461 Pericles dominates Athenian political life for the following 32 years 431 Start of the Peloponnesian War between Athens and Sparta, which lasts until 404 405 Denys becomes tyrant of Syracuse (Sicily) · 4004 Hegemony of Sparta over the Hellenic world 381 Celts sack Rome 359 Philip of Macedonia rises to the throne of Macedonia, which becomes an important power 348 Second treaty between Rome and Carthage 336 Assasination of Philip of Macedonia in Greece. His son, Alexander III the Great, succeeds him.
331 to 301 323 Death of Alexander in Babylon. Ptolemy alloted Egyptian satrap (provincial governor). Ptolemy annexes Palestine, Syria and Syro-Phoenicia 311 Ptolemy marries Berenice and proclaims himself Ptolemy I Soter in 304 approx. 309 Birth of Ptolemy II Philadelphus 301 Ptolemy attacks Jerusalem, regains Judaea	**331 to 301** 304 approx. Cult of Serapis, hybrid Greco-Egyptian god, introduced to Egypt by Ptolemy I.	**331 to 301** 326 Alexander III the Great defeats King Poros of India 321 Defeat of the Romans by the Samnites 306 Third treaty between Rome and Carthage. It recognizes the hegemony of Rome over Italy and of Carthage over Sicily
300 to 271 Ptolemy II marries and divorces Arsinoë I, marries his own sister Arsinoë II 289 Death of Ptolemy I, Ptolemy II becomes sole king	**300 to 271** With the arrival of the Ptolemys, important agricultural innovations including biannual harvests Settling of Greek colonies in Egypt	**300 to 271** 294 Re-establishment of democracy in Athens 290 Rome conquers central Italy (Latium, Etruia, Campanie) 280 Celtic (Galatian) invasion of Macedonia and Thrace

HISTORY	EGYPTIAN SOCIETY	AROUND EGYPT

270 to 241
268 Death and deification of Arnoë II
246 Death of Ptolemy II, accession of Ptolemy III Euergates

240 to 201
222 Death of Ptolemy III Euergates. Accession of Ptolemy IV Philopator
217 Ptolemy IV marries Arsinoë III
Native uprisings in Upper Egypt
210 Birth of Ptolemy V
205 Secession in Upper Egypt
204 Death of Ptolemy IV
203 Regency of Agathocles

200 to 145
186(c.) Recapture of Thebes, end of secession in Upper Egypt
181 Death of Ptolemy V Epiphanes, regency of Cleopatra I
176 Death of Cleopatra I, accession of Ptolemy VI as minor
167 Conflict between Ptolemy VI and Ptolemy VIII, co-regent
164 Exile of Ptolemy VIII
145 Ptolemy VI killed in battle, Ptolemy VII returns to Alexandria to rule with Cleopatra II and Ptolemy VII

144 to 101
Ptolemy VIII murders Ptolemy VII, is enthroned as Pharoah at Memphis
143 Purge of Alexandrian intellectuals
132 Cleopatra II raises revolt against Ptolemy VIII and becomes sole ruler
Return of Ptolemy VIII and beginning of civil war
128 Cleopatra flees to Syria
124 Reconciliation of Cleopatra II and Ptolemy VII, general amnesties in Egypt
116 Death of Ptolemy VIII, joint rule of Ptolemy IX and Cleopatra III
Cleopatra III forces Ptolemy IX out of Egypt
107 Ptolemy X arrives from Cyprus to assume trone
103 or 102 Cleopatra II drives Ptolemy X from Alexandria
Ptolemy X returns, murders Cleopatra II, marries Cleopatra Berenice

100 to 51
87 Ptolemy X and Cleopatra Berenice expelled from Alexandria. Ptolemy IX recovers the throne
Death of Ptolemy X in a naval battle off Cyprus; return from exile of Cleopatra Berenice as joint ruler

---

270 to 201
Searching for combat elephants, exploration of Eastern Africa
297 Foundation of Museum and Alexandria Library. Zenodotus is named head of the library
285 Sostratus of Cnidus establishes plans for the Lighthouse of Alexandria. The Greek astronomer Aristarchus of Samos resides in Alexandria
246 The Greek mathematician and astronomer Eratosthenes is named head of the Alexandria Library

200 to 145
196 Decree of the Rosetta Stone by Ptolemy V: official decrees are hereafter written in 3 languages: hieroglyphic, demotic and Greek. Death of Eratosthenes. Aristophanes of Byzantium succeeds him as head of the Alexandria Library

144 to 101
117 Discovery of monsoon route from Egypt to India

100 to 51
Greek influence starts to be visible on Alexandrian monuments
60 The Greek historian, Diodorus Siculus tells of seeing a Roman lynched for killing a cat

---

270 to 241
270 Complete Roman hegemony of meridional Italy
264 First Punic War between Carthage and Rome, Rome defeats Carthage in 239
247 Birth of Hannibal in Carthage

240 to 201
237 Lead by Hamilcar, the Carthaginian army conquers Spain
219 Beginning of the second Punic War which lasts 17 years
218 With 50,000 men, 9,000 cavaliers and 37 elephants, Hannibal crosses the Pyrenees, and then the Alps

200 to 145
160 At Pergamum, founding of library second only to Alexandria's. Antony will offer 20,000 of its books to Cleopatra
149 Third Punic War between Rome and Carthage, which ends in 146 with Carthage's complete defeat

144 to 101
125 To protect Marseille, Rome conquers all of Gaul to the meridional Pyrenees
106 Birth of Pompei in Rome. His son-in-law and later his enemy
105 Invasion of Gaul by Barbarians. Rome tries to stop them
101 Birth of Julius Caesar

100 to 51
91 The Italian peninsula is first called Italy
Civil War in Italy until 82, which concludes with the dictatorship of Sylla
88 Greece revolts against Rome
73 to 71 Revolt of slaves in Rome, lead by Spartacus

HISTORY	EGYPTIAN SOCIETY	AROUND EGYPT
81 Death of Ptolemy IX. Cleopatra Berenice is sole ruler 80 Ptolemy XI Alexander II proclaimed king of Egypt, marries Cleopatra Berenice, murders her, is lynched by mob 80 Ptolemy IX's illegitimate son, Ptolemy XII Auletes, seizes throne and marries his sister, Cleopatra V 59 Ptolemy XII driven out of Alexandria 57 Death of Cleopatra V 55 Romans restore Ptolemy XII to throne 51 Death of Ptolemy XII, Ptolemy XIII marries his sister, Cleopatra VII, and they become joint rulers		63 Cicero consulate of Rome; Pompei takes Jerusalem, Palestine under Roman domination 58 Beginning of the Gallic war. Julius Caeser leads the Roman army
50 to 41 Cleopatra VII at war with her brother Ptolemy XIII Cleopatra VII leaves for Thebaid 48 Pompey reaches Alexandria, where he is assassinated 47 Julius Caesar arrives in Egypt with 4,000 men Birth of Ptolemy XV, called Caesarion, to Caesar and Cleopatra 44 Death of Caesar, Cleopatra returns to Alexandria from Rome 41 to 40 Marc Antony meets Cleopatra at Tarsus, winters with her in Alexandria, Cleopatra bears Antony twins	**50 to 41** 49 Drought in Egypt 47 Fire in the Alexandria Library Ban on shipping of grain to Egypt, with the exception of Alexandria 43 Famine and plague	**50 to 41** 50 Gaul becomes a Roman province 47 Caesar arrives in Alexandria 44 Caesar bestows upon himself the title of imperator in perpetuity. He is assassinated on the ides of March 43 Civil War in Rome between Marc Antony, Caesar's lieutenant, backed by the majority; and Octavius, backed by the Senate. This war lasts until 30 and ends with the victoy of Octavius
40 to 30 37 Antony winters in Athens with his wife Octavia, Octavian's sister Antony marries Cleopatra in Antioch, acknowledges their children 34 Antony's triumph in Egypt 32 Antony and Cleopatra winter in Ephesus, Octavia divorces Antony 31 Octavian opposes Antony at sea battle of Actium, defeats him 30 Antony and Cleopatra commit suicide as Octavian enters Alexandria, Octavian has Caesarion killed, end of Ptolemaic Dynasty	**40 to 29** 29 Introduction of Julian calendar by Emperor Augustus	**40 to 27** 40 Heroditus I is named King of Judaea by the Romans and takes control of Jerusalem. 27 Octavius receives the title of Augustus from the Senate; end of Roman Repulic and beginning of Roman Empire.

CHRONOLOGY AND DEVELOPMENT OF ARCHITECTURE IN EGYPT

Before Jesus Christ – 3000

End of the pre-Pharaonic period. Founding of the kingdom of Egypt *Kemet* (The Black Country) following the unification of Upper and Lower Egypt by King Menes. The Egyptians practice handicrafts, stock rearing and agriculture. Limited use of locally-mined metals (gold, copper).

- 2920 – 2575

● *1st, 2nd and 3rd Dynasties.*
Constitution of the Pharaonic political system and development of hieroglyphic script. Civil architecture is made up of perishable materials (wood, reeds, unfired bricks) but the royal palace pattern persists in funerary architecture. The latter is organised in the form of broad rectangular tombs with superstructures of unfired brick (e.g. the mastaba at Saqqara dating from the 1st Dynasty and attributed to Queen Merneith). Tombs are built on the plateau at Saqqara, opposite the capital, Memphis. Cenotaphs (imitation tombs) are constructed for sovereigns at the holy city of Abydos, sacred to the god Osiris. Royal architecture in this period already shows a clear tendency toward monumentality.

The first architectural ensemble built of standardized small bricks was the funerary complex of the pharaoh Djeser (2630–2611) built by the architect Imhotep at Saqqara. This complex includes the first step pyramid. The use of limestone in construction made possible a culturally-refined palace architecture of wood and brick.

- 2575 – 2150

● *The 4th, 5th and 6th Dynasties.*
OLD KINGDOM.
Period of political centralisation. Trend away from the step pyramid toward the double-sloped pyramid, which becomes straight during the reign of Snofru, father of Cheops. The classical funerary complexes, made up of a single tomb beneath a pyramid and of two temples linked by a covered path (an upper funerary temple and a lower 'reception' temple) began to appear at the beginning of the 4th Dynasty. Construction of the Great Pyramid of Giza by Cheops, Chephren and Mycerinus. Construction of the Sphinx in the reign of

Djedef-Re, son of Cheops, and creation of the Great Sphinx of Giza in the reign of Chephren. Development of the sun cult with the emergence of the demi-god of Heliopolis, Khepri-Re-Atum. Construction of sun temples during the 5th Dynasty, with central monuments already taking the form of obelisks (Temple of Sahure). Compilation of the *Pyramid Texts*,  used for the burial of monarchs. A number of private mastabas, built for important figures in the hierarchy, were built on the plateaus of Giza and Saqqara. Their sculpted and painted decors depict images of daily life and funeral scenes. Decadence of the political system during the long reign of Pepy II at the close of the 6th Dynasty.

- 2150 – 2040

● *7th, 8th, 9th and 10th Dynasties.* **FIRST INTERMEDIATE PERIOD.**
This period of local anarchy and disintegration of pharaonic power – when political and economic power was concentrated in the hands of hereditary regional princes, called *nomarchs* – coincided with the appearance of the provincial necropolis. The tombs dug in the cliff-faces of Middle Egypt for the *nomarchs* were painted with scenes which departed from the stricter conventions of the Old Kingdom. The general pessimism of the epoch is very evident in its beautiful literary compositions (*The Desperate Man's Dialogue With His Soul*).

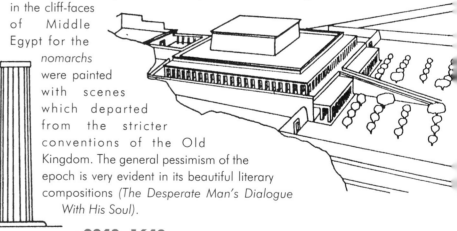

- 2040, 1640

● *9th, 12th, 13th and 14th Dynasties.* **MIDDLE KINGDOM.**
Reunification of Egypt by Nebhepetre Mentuhotep, prince of Thebes and founder of the 11th Dynasty. Thebes, an ordinary provincial town, became the capital of Egypt. The sovereign broke with the funerary tradition of the Old Kingdom by building his funerary temple at Thebes, instead of at Memphis. His temple of Deir el-Bahari

inaugurated an apparently new form of terraced architecture. The Theban sovereigns of the 12th Dynasty returned to the north and set up their administrative capital at Ity-Taouy, facing Licht. Their pyramids made of smaller bricks (unlike the Great Pyramids of Giza) are now in a very dilapidated condition. Amenomhat III, the last great monarch of this period, brought the concept of the funerary temple to its highest form with his creation of the Labyrinth of Hawara. New conquests in Nubia led to the construction of fortresses of unfired brick in the area south of Aswan. Regional princes continued to be buried near their capital, in hypogeums that echoed domestic norms of architecture. The *Pyramid Texts* evolved into the *Sarcophagus Texts*, used for the greatest officials of the realm. In addition, a number of classical texts were written at this time, notably *Amenemhat I's Instructions to his son, Sesostris I* and *The Adventures of Sinuhe*, the first novel in recorded history. The many royal foundations, temples and chapels built at this time are now represented by no more than a few monuments (Chapel of Sesostris I at Karnak, Temple of Amenemhat III at Medinet Mahdi). Most of these temples were dismantled for re use under the New Kingdom, nevertheless there is a technical perfection and elegance of proportion about them which cannot be mistaken. They coincided with the appearance of the first brick pylons on either side of monumental gateways. Sesostris I inaugurated the first obelisk on the edge of the oasis of the Fayum (the obelisk of Begig). Egypt experienced a further period of political instability towards the close of the 12th Dynasty.

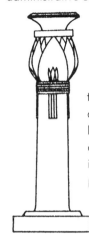

-1640 – 1550:

● *15th, 16th and 17th Dynasties.*
SECOND INTERMEDIATE PERIOD.
Invasion of the Delta by the Hyksos from Palestine. The wheel appears in Egypt.

The princes of Thebes lead the progressive reconquest of Northern Egypt, and once again have themselves buried in hypogeums, close to the Valley of the Kings.

- 1550 – 1070

● *18th, 19th and 20th Dynasties.*
NEW KINGDOM.
Reunification of Egypt by Amosis, prince of Thebes. Thebes recovers its status as a capital of Egypt, along with Memphis. The kingdom becomes immensely wealthy, on account of a series of conquests in Palestine, Syria and Nubia. Development of Egyptian chariot forces. Major architectural projects are initiated. The Temple of Amon at Thebes is regularly enlarged; the power of its clergy grows apace.

The architectural influence of the 11th and 12th Dynasties remains considerable during the first half of the 18th Dynasty (Temple of Hatchepsut at Deir el-Bahari, in imitation of that of Montuhotep).

Inauguration of the Valley of the Kings as the principal royal cemetery. Pyramid-shaped tombs are dug under the hills at Thebes; subsequently, larger and larger funerary temples are built into this hill, facing the capital (Amenophis III's 'Temple of a Million Years'; the funerary Temple of Rameses II). Construction of the Temple of Luxor. Major works are initiated in all the important cities of Egypt, notably at Abydos. Monumental pylons and obelisks proliferate in the various sanctuaries, which become progressively larger in size. Reappearance of open solar temples, reaching its apogee under the reign of Amenophis IV – Akhenaton, with the cult of the god Aton. Rameses II transfers the capital to Per-Rameses (The House of Rameses) in the Eastern Delta, displacing a number of monuments dating from earlier epochs (12th and 18th Dynasties). Construction of the Temple of Abu Simbel, south of Aswan, to the glory of Rameses II. Rameses III, the last major monarch of the New Kingdom, builds the last of the great funerary temples at Medinet Habu.

- 1070 – 712

- *21st, 22nd, 23rd and 24 Dynasties.*
  THIRD INTERMEDIATE PERIOD.

Partition of Egypt between the High Priests of Amon, at Thebes, and the sovereigns installed at Tanis. The new capital of the delta re-utilises the monuments of Per-Rameses. At Thebes, residual development of the major architectural programmes of the New Kingdom. Construction of annexes to the great temples, and construction of chapels under the authority of the Adorers of Amon at Thebes. First mention of the Island of Pharos, in the *Iliad* of Homer. The Nubian King Piankhi launches a major campaign of reconquest from Napata, in Nubia, as far as Memphis. Egypt submits to the new pharaoh.

- 712 – 332

- *25th, 26th, 27th, 28th, 29th and 30th Dynasties.*
  LOW PERIOD.

The Nubian sovereigns reign from Memphis. New construction activities in Upper Egypt (colonnade of Taharqa within the precinct of the Temple of Amon at Thebes). Assyrian invasion and sack of Thebes circa 660. Psammetichus I founds the 26th Dynasty, called the Saite Dynasty on account of its origin at Sais in the Delta. Under the reign of his successors, architectural programmes become more ambitious, largely due to political and economic stability. Egypt opens to the Mediterranean. The pharaohs begin to use Greek mercenaries. The royal architecture of this time, which was concentrated in the Delta, has now vanished. Nechao II undertakes the building of the first Suez Canal. Foundation of Naucratis, a Greek city of the western Delta. Establishment of Greek colonies, notably at

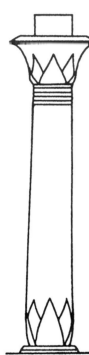

Memphis. During the period of the first Persian Domination (17th Dynasty), construction of the Temple of Hibis at the Khargeh Oasis. Completion of the Suez Canal by Darius. Nectanebo I is the last great native Egyptian monarch, during whose reign a large number of constructions are undertaken. The second Persian Domination, beginning in about 343, ushers in a period of oppression. Aristotle becomes the tutor of Alexander, the son of Philip II of Macedonia, in 343.

- 332 – 30

- *Reigns of Alexander the Great, then of Alexander's general Ptolomy I Soter and his descendants.*
  PTOLEMAIC EPOCH.

Alexander the Great invades Egypt and liberates it from Persian domination. He founds Alexandria, but is buried at Memphis. His remains are later transferred to Alexandria. The Ptolemies relaunch the construction of temples dedicated to Egyptian gods, notably in Upper Egypt (Temple of Hathor at Dendera, Temple of Horus at Edfou). The great animal necropolises reach their apogee (Bubasteion and Serapeum at Saqqara). First appearance of composite orders of columns. Decadence of the art of bas-relief. Under the reigns of Ptolemy II Philadelphus and Arsinoe II, creation of the principal monuments of Alexandria; the Museum, the Library and the Pharos.

From 30 BC

- **ROMAN EPOCH.**

Egypt becomes a Roman province. Temples already begun are completed, and new ones founded (Temple of Khnum at Dom Ombo). Minor additions to existing buildings (Tower of Trajan at Philae). In 395 AD, division of the Empire between East (capital: Byzantium) and West (capital: Rome). Egypt is integrated into the Byzantine Empire.

THE GREEK WORLD

Before Jesus Christ – 1500

First signs of monumental architecture at Mycenae (cyclopean walls, tombs and palaces). Appearance of the *megaron*, a rectangular central hall with a vestibule, fronted by a porch resting on two columns.

– 900

Development of the geometrical style. First absidal chapels.

– 800

Search for architectural solutions in the use of perishable materials (wood). Limestone and marble have not yet been mastered as construction materials. Oriental and Egyptian influences appear in Greek art. Chapels, close in design to domestic architecture, become known as repositories for terra-cotta ex-votos (ex-voto of the Heraion of Argos). The temple is recognised as the house of one or other of the gods. It has an altar outside it which is used for sacrifices, and its principal function is to house the statue of a divinity.

– 776

Inauguration of the Olympic Games. Creation of the first Heraion of Olympia.

– 700

Development of the rectangular temple constructed on a stylobate, with an axial colonnade supporting a roof with two slopes (Temple of Apollo at Thermon, circa 630) The temple of Hera at Argos is surrounded by a wooden colonnade and thus becomes one of the first peripteral temples.

– 650

Short-lived injection of Oriental influence, with the foundation of the temple of Prinias in Crete.

– 621

Draco begins framing a new code of law for Athens.

– 600

Foundation of Marseille by the Phoceans. Emergence of the Doric Order in continental Greece, Southern Italy and

Sicily, representing the transfer of an architectural technique from wood to stone. First Doric temples (Temple of Artemis at Corfu).

– 561

Peisistratos becomes tyrant of Athens. Croesus is king of Lydia. Embellishment of Greek city-states by local tyrants. Development of forms of civil and military architecture marking the political independence of the city-states (fountains, fortifications, theatres, agoras). In Asia Minor, experiments in decoration lead to the creation of the Ionic Order, heavily ornamental in character and inspired by the world of plant life.

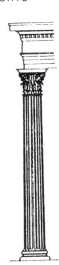

– 530 – 500

End of the tyrannies. Construction of the Temple of Apollo at Corinth. Construction of treasuries - votive monuments raised by the cities within the sanctuaries of Apollo at Delphi and Zeus at Olympia. (Treasury of the Siphnians at Delphi in 525). First temple of Athena on the Acropolis at Athens. Invention of the Corinthian Order, attributed to the sculptor and architect Kallimachos; this was in fact an adaptation of the Ionic Order. The difference was that allowed no angles on the capital, a considerable visual improvement.

– 490 – 480

The Persian Wars. Battle of Marathon (490).

– 470

Creation of the Auriga of Polyzalos at Delphi.

– 461

Pericles becomes the leader of the democrats in Athens. Development of the city. Systematic use of the colonnaded portico (stoa) for a variety of functions. Creation of stadiums, odeons, assembly halls (Bouleuterion at Athens). Construction of the Temple of Zeus at Olympia.

– 448 – 430

Construction of the Parthenon by Pheidias and Iktinos. Creation of the chryselephantine statue of Athena Parthenos by Pheidias. Creation of the Discobolos by Myron.

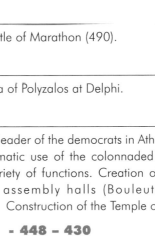

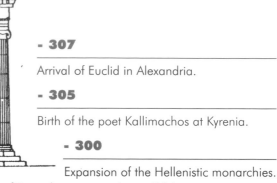

- 431 – 407

War between Athens and Sparta. Construction of the Erechtheion. Death of Pericles in 429.

- 386

Greek expansion in the Adriatic and into Corsica.

- 377

Mausolus becomes satrap of Caria. Monumental tombs proliferate in Asia Minor, while continental Greece continues to favour tombs set beneath tumuli.

- 376

Athenian domination of the Aegean.

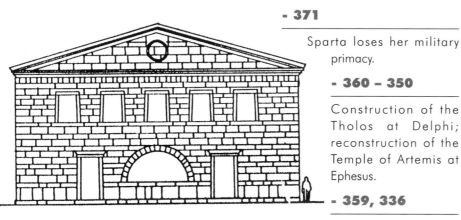

- 371

Sparta loses her military primacy.

- 360 – 350

Construction of the Tholos at Delphi; reconstruction of the Temple of Artemis at Ephesus.

- 359, 336

Reign of Philip II, father of Alexander, in Macedon. Philip is assassinated.

- 336, 323

Alexander the Great, King of Macedon, conquers Asia Minor, Syria and Egypt.

- 331

Foundation of Alexandria by Democrates of Rhodes and Kleomenes of Naucratis on a basic rectangular grill plan. Susa, Babylon and Persepolis fall to the armies of Alexander. Sculpture of the Apollo of the Belvedere.

- 326

Alexander's fleet enters the Indian Ocean.

- 323

Death of Alexander followed by the division of his empire among his generals. Construction of the Theatre of Epidauros.

- 307

Arrival of Euclid in Alexandria.

- 305

Birth of the poet Kallimachos at Kyrenia.

- 300

Expansion of the Hellenistic monarchies. The growing power of Rome begins to make itself felt.

- 246

The Greek mathematician and astronomer Eratosthenes takes control of the Library of Alexandria, proves that the world is round, and calculates its radius.

- 211

Rome seizes Syracuse.

- 190

Construction of the Victory of Samothrace.

- 167

Decline of Rhodes.

- 147 – 146

War of the Achaean League against Rome. Rome prevails. Destruction of Carthage, sack of Corinth.

- 133

Attalos III bequeaths the kingdom of Pergamum to Rome.

- 129

Greece becomes a Roman province of Asia.

- 88

Revolt of the Greeks.

- 87

Athens falls to the Roman army.

- 47

Julius Caesar, after defeating Pharnakes at the battle of Zela, pronounces the famous words 'Veni, vidi, vici'. Burning of the Library of Alexandria.

Before Jesus Christ – 753

The city of Rome is formed from a conglomeration of villages built on the hills overlooking the Tiber.

- 600

The Etruscan civilisation reaches its high water mark. Etruscan princes annex Latium. In Rome, the draining of the Pontine marshes clears the way for the construction of a political centre, the Forum. The Etruscans build the first monuments in the city.

- 509

Founding of the Capitol. Expulsion of the Etruscan kings; founding of the Roman republic.

- 500 – 200

The population of Rome grows very quickly. Temples are built either on the Etruscan model, or in imitation of the Greek temples of Southern Italy and Sicily. The Gauls invade Italy in 390.

- 264 – 202

First and Second Punic Wars. Gradual conquest of the Greek world. Colonisation of the Mediterranean basin.

- 149 – 146

Third Punic War. Complete Roman victory over Carthage.

1st century BC

Development of Roman town planning. Reconstruction of the Sanctuary of Fortune at Palestrina, the first major architectural undertaking in Roman history. Architectural development of theatres erected in several tiers of arcades, rather than cut into hillsides.

- 49 – 44

Dictatorship of Caesar. Construction of the Forum of Caesar and the temple of Venus Genitrix.

- 31

Battle of Actium.

- 29

Creation of the first monumental triumphal arch, a descendant of the fornices of the 2nd century BC, in the Forum at Rome. Glorification of the emperor by the city's monuments. Founding of the Temple of Apollo Palatine, as a memorial to the battle of Actium.

- 27

Octavius adopts the title of Augustus.

- 20

Construction of the Pont du Gard, the Nîmes aqueduct, at the direction of Agrippa. Founding of the Maison Carrée, the principal monument in the forum at Nimes. The temple was Corinthian Greek in design, though raised on an Etruscan-style podium.

- 14 – 37 AD

Reign of Tiberius. Completion of the Theatre of Lepcis Magna. Founding of the Triumphal Arch at Orange and the Temple of Baal at Palmyra, a syncretism between Roman and Mesopotamian architecture.

- 79

Destruction of Pompeii and Herculaneum following the eruption of Vesuvius.

- 80

Inauguration of the Coliseum, the model for all Roman amphitheatres.

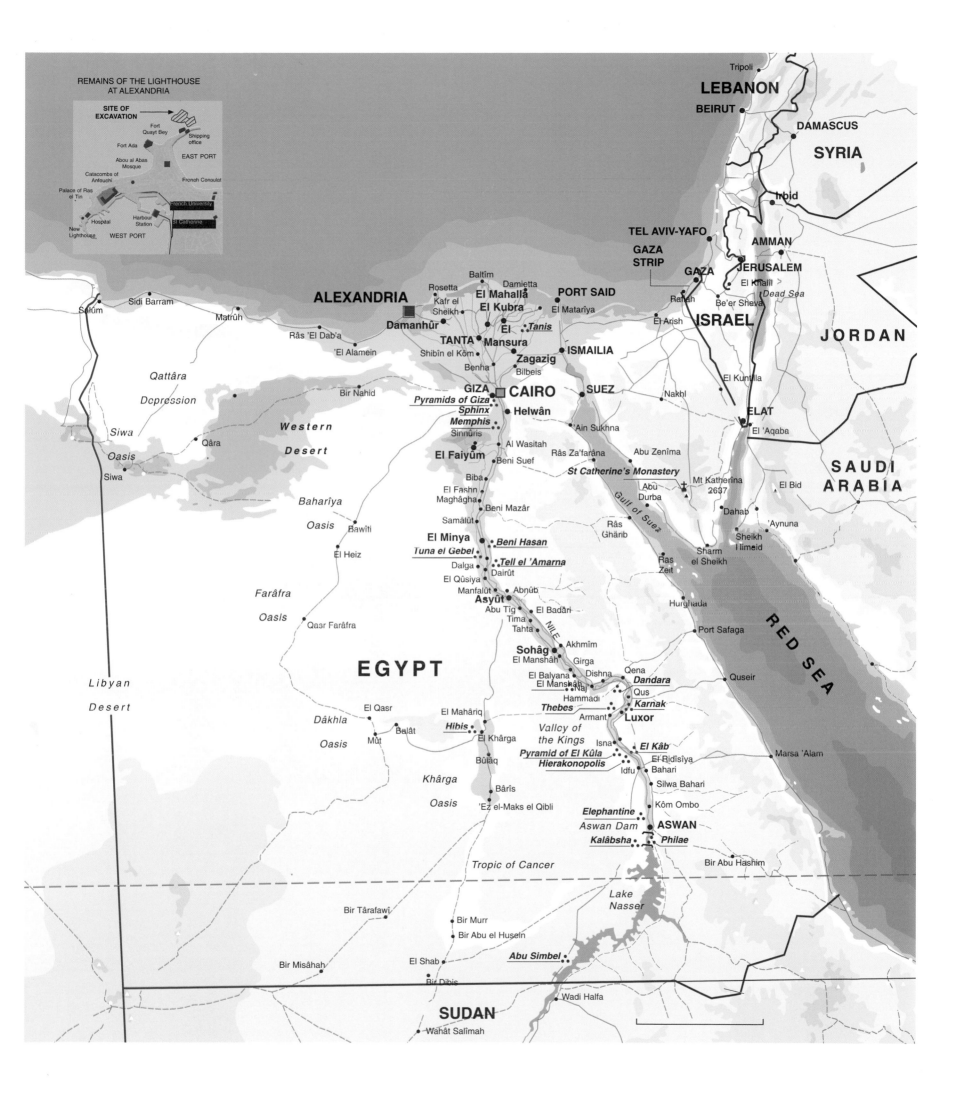

REMAINS OF THE LIGHTHOUSE AT ALEXANDRIA

SITE OF EXCAVATION

Fort Quayt Bey
Fort Ada
Shipping office
Abou al Abas Mosque
EAST PORT
Catacombs of Anfouchi
French Consulat
Palace of Ras el Tin
French University
Hospital
Harbour Station
St Catherine
New Lighthouse
WEST PORT

Tripoli

LEBANON

BEIRUT

DAMASCUS

SYRIA

Irbid

TEL AVIV-YAFO

GAZA STRIP

AMMAN

GAZA

JERUSALEM

El Khalil

Dead Sea

Rafah

Be'er Sheva

ISRAEL

JORDAN

Salûm

Sîdi Barram

Matrûh

Râs 'El Dab'a

'El Alamein

El Arish

El Kuntilla

Rosetta

Baltîm

Damietta

ALEXANDRIA

Kafr el Sheikh

El Mahallā El Kubra

PORT SAID

El Matarîya

ELAT

El 'Aqaba

Damanhûr

El

Tanis

TANTA

Mansura

ISMAILIA

Shibîn el Kôm

Zagazig

Benha

Bilbeis

Qattâra

Depression

Bir Nahid

GIZA

CAIRO

SUEZ

Nakhl

'Ain Sukhna

ELAT

Pyramids of Giza

Helwân

Sphinx

Memphis

Sinnûris

Al Wasitah

Râs Za'farâna

Abu Zenîma

El Faiyûm

Beni Suef

St Catherine's Monastery

Abû Durba

Mt Katherîna 2637

El Bid

Siwa

Oasis

Siwa

Qâra

Western Desert

Biba

El Fashn

Maghâgha

Baharîya

Oasis

Bawîti

Beni Mazâr

Samâlût

Râs Ghârib

Dahab

'Aynuna

Sheikh Humeid

El Heiz

El Minya

Beni Hasan

Tuna el Gebel

Tell el 'Amarna

Dalga

Dairût

Ras Zeit

Sharm el Sheikh

Farâfra

Oasis

El Qûsiya

Manfalût

Abnûb

Qasr Farâfra

Asyût

Abu Tîg

El Badâri

Hurghada

RED SEA

Tîma

Tahta

Port Safaga

Libyan

Desert

El Qasr

El Mahârîq

Sohâg

El Manshâh

Akhmîm

Girga

Quseir

EGYPT

Balât

Hibis

El Khârga

El Balyana

El Manshâh

Dishna

Qena

Dandara

Marsa 'Alam

Dâkhla

Oasis

Mût

Hammadi

Naj

Qus

Karnak

Thebes

Armant

Luxor

Bûlâq

Bârîs

Valley of the Kings

Isna

El Kâb

El Ridîsîya

Bahari

Idfu

Pyramid of El Kûla

Hierakonopolis

Khârga

Oasis

'Ez el-Maks el Qibli

Silwa Bahari

Kôm Ombo

Elephantine

Aswan Dam

ASWAN

Kalâbsha

Philae

Tropic of Cancer

Bir Abu Hashim

Bir Târafawî

Lake Nasser

Bir Murr

Bir Abu el Husein

El Shab

Abu Simbel

Bir Misâhah

Bir Dibis

Wadi Halfa

SUDAN

Wahât Salîmah

BIBLIOGRAPHICAL REFERENCES

Page 9 : The poem 'God abandons Anthony' is extracted from *Poèmes anciens ou retrouvés* by Constantin Cavafy, translated by Gilles Ortlieb and Pierre Leyris, Seghers 1978.

Page 39 : The quotation from Achille Tatius is extracted from *Aventures de Leucippé et Clitophon* (Book V), in *Romanciers grecs et latins*, text edited and translated by Pierre Grimal, Bibliothèque de La Pléiade, Gallimard 1958.

Page 51 : The quotation from Ibn Jubair is extracted from *Relation de voyages* ('De Grenade en Egypte'), in *Voyageurs Arabes*, translated by Paule Charles-Dominique, Bibliothèque de la Pléiade, Gallimard 1995.

Page 52 : The quotation from Ibn Battuta is extracted from *Voyages et périples* ('L'Egypte'), in *Voyageurs Arabes*, translated by Paule Charles-Dominique, Bibliothèque de la Pléiade, Gallimard 1995.

Pages 52 and **54** : The quotation from Homer is extracted from *The Odyssey* (Part IV), translated by Louis Bardollet, Laffont 1995.

Pages 54 and **55** : The poem ' Sur la mort d'Arsinoë' is extracted from *Épigrammes, hymnes* of Callimaque, text edited and translated by Emile Cahen, Les Belles Lettres, 1925.

ACKNOWLEDGMENTS

This book was produced with the help of :

The French Institute of Oriental Archaeology (IFAO)
The Centre for Alexandrian Studies (CEA)
The Supreme Council for Egyptian Antiquities
Gédéon
The Elf Foundation
The EdF Foundation
Leica France
The European Institute of Underwater Archaeology
Press Agency SYGMA

Photographic Credits

Photographs by Stéphane Compoint / SYGMA
pages 14-15, 55, 61: Jean Louis Leibovitch / Gédéon ; page 30: Dagli Orti ;
page 44: Jean-Claude Golvin; page 50: CEA-IFAO ; pages 82-83: Gédéon / Ex Machina

Architectural chronologies and drawings by Roselyne Cepko
Map by Antoine Capelle

Typeset by Dupont Photogravure

First published in 1996 as *Alexandrie: Septième Merveille du Monde*
by Editions Robert Laffont, S.A.
24 avenue Marceau
75381 Paris

First published in the UK in 1996 by
George Weidenfeld and Nicolson Ltd
The Orion Publishing Group
Orion House
5 Upper St Martin's Lane
London WC2H 9EA

Text © William La Riche
Photography © Stéphane Compoint / SYGMA

ISBN 0 297 82180 6

A catalogue record is available for this book from the British Library

N° d'éditeur : 37180-63
Imprimé par Clerc S.A. - 18200 Saint-Amand